EDUCATION AND LEARNING TO THINK

LAUREN B. RESNICK

Committee on Mathematics, Science, and
Technology Education

Commission on Behavioral and Social Sciences and Education

National Research Council

NATIONAL ACADEMY PRESS
Washington, D.C. 1987

National Academy Press   2101 Constitution Avenue, NW   Washington, DC 20418

NOTICE: The project that is the subject of this report was approved by the Governing Board of the National Research Council, whose members are drawn from the councils of the National Academy of Sciences, the National Academy of Engineering, and the Institute of Medicine. The members of the committee responsible for the report were chosen for their special competences and with regard for appropriate balance.

This report has been reviewed by a group other than the author according to procedures approved by a Report Review Committee consisting of members of the National Academy of Sciences, the National Academy of Engineering, and the Institute of Medicine.

The National Academy of Sciences is a private, nonprofit, self-perpetuating society of distinguished scholars engaged in scientific and engineering research, dedicated to the furtherance of science and technology and to their use for the general welfare. Upon the authority of the charter granted to it by the Congress in 1863, the Academy has a mandate that requires it to advise the federal government on scientific and technical matters. Dr. Frank Press is president of the National Academy of Sciences.

The National Academy of Engineering was established in 1964, under the charter of the National Academy of Sciences, as a parallel organization of outstanding engineers. It is autonomous in its administration and in the selection of its members, sharing with the National Academy of Sciences the responsibility for advising the federal government. The National Academy of Engineering also sponsors engineering programs aimed at meeting national needs, encourages education and research, and recognizes the superior achievements of engineers. Dr. Robert M. White is president of the National Academy of Engineering.

The Institute of Medicine was established in 1970 by the National Academy of Sciences to secure the services of eminent members of appropriate professions in the examination of policy matters pertaining to the health of the public. The Institute acts under the responsibility given to the National Academy of Sciences by its congressional charter to be an adviser to the federal government and, upon its own initiative, to identify issues of medical care, research, and education. Dr. Samuel O. Thier is president of the Institute of Medicine.

The National Research Council was organized by the National Academy of Sciences in 1916 to associate the broad community of science and technology with the Academy's purposes of furthering knowledge and advising the federal government. Functioning in accordance with general policies determined by the Academy, the Council has become the principal operating agency of both the National Academy of Sciences and the National Academy of Engineering in providing services to the government, the public, and the scientific and engineering communities. The Council is administered jointly by both Academies and the Institute of Medicine. Dr. Frank Press and Dr. Robert M. White are chairman and vice chairman, respectively, of the National Research Council.

Library of Congress Catalog Card Number 87- 43107

ISBN 0-309-03785-9
First Printing, October 1987
Second Printing, January 1989
Third Printing, May 1989
Fourth Printing, November 1989
Fifth Printing, January 1991
Sixth Printing, July 1991
Seventh Printing, January 1992

Printed in the United States of America

Foreword

The Committee on Research in Mathematics, Science, and Education was established in the Commission on Behavioral and Social Sciences and Education of the National Research Council in 1984 in response to a request from the U.S. Department of Education. Its initial tasks, for that department and the National Science Foundation, were to develop a set of research priorities and to consider the role of multidisciplinary research for science, mathematics, and technology education. That work resulted in two reports, *Mathematics, Science, and Technology Education: A Research Agenda* (National Academy Press, 1985) and *Interdisciplinary Research in Science, Mathematics, and Technology Education* (National Academy Press, 1987).

While preparing the first report, the committee became interested in exploring in more depth two issues: how the school environment can be manipulated to maximize opportunities for children to succeed in learning science and mathematics, and how children learn reasoning and other complex thinking skills. Work on the first issue was carried out by Michael Cole, Peg Griffen, and their colleagues at the Laboratory of Comparative Human Cognition at the University of California at San Diego; their monograph *Contextual Factors in Education: Improving Science and Mathematics Education for Minorities and Women* was published by and is available from the Wisconsin Center for Education Research, Madison, Wisconsin. Work on the second issue was undertaken by Lauren Resnick at the Learning Research and Development Center of the University of Pittsburgh and resulted in this special monograph. Carnegie Corporation of New York is generously supporting the distribution of both volumes.

Preface

This paper addresses the question of what American schools can do to more effectively teach what have come to be called "higher order skills." Unlike most National Research Council documents, it is not so much a report as the result of extended reflection upon a set of questions raised by and about the nation's educational system. This reflection has received the guidance and critique of a splendid working group of psychologists, educators, computer scientists, and philosophers:

Carl Bereiter, Department of Applied Cognitive Science, Ontario Institute for Studies in Education

John Bransford, Department of Psychology and Director, Learning Technology Center, Vanderbilt University

Ann L. Brown, Center for the Study of Reading, University of Illinois

Jerome S. Bruner, Department of Psychology, New School for Social Research

Susan Carey, Department of Psychology, Massachusetts Institute of Technology

Allan Collins, Bolt Beranek and Newman, Inc., Cambridge, Mass.

Robert H. Ennis, College of Education, University of Illinois

David Perkins, Graduate School of Education, Harvard University and

Roger Schank, Department of Computer Science, Yale University.

The working group exchanged written statements and participated in a two-day meeting in Washington, D.C., in the fall of 1984, during which the issues raised in the written statements were discussed at length. Members of the group also provided guidance in finding and interpreting information relevant to its concerns. Most important, members of the working group responded to drafts of this paper; these responses have been of great value in shaping the final version. However, what follows is not a group report, but a personal distillation of the working group's wisdom and advice. It should be read and used with that understanding.

Several individuals in addition to members of the working group have been generous with their time and ideas. I would like to mention two in particular, Carol Dweck of the University of Illinois and Mark Lepper of Stanford University. Thanks are also due to the many who sent materials about their own and others' work on the teaching of higher order skills and who were willing to talk with me and, in many cases, to comment on an early draft of this paper. A list of the individuals who responded to requests for information and ideas appears in the appendix.

Finally, special thanks are due to Senta Raizen, study director of the Committee on Research in Mathematics, Science, and Technology Education, for her organization of the initial working group and overall management of the project. Not least among her contributions was securing support for this effort from the Carnegie Corporation of New York, whose contribution is hereby thankfully acknowledged.

LAUREN RESNICK
Learning Research and
Development Center
University of Pittsburgh

Contents

Education and Learning to Think

INTRODUCTION

The question of whether schools can do a better job of teaching American children "higher order skills" is very much in the air. It arises in Congressional hearings, where calls are heard for school graduates better able to take on work that requires responsibility and judgment. It is reflected in public concern that changing employment demands are not being met, students' preparation for college is less than satisfactory, and general problem-solving abilities remain low. Yet beyond the agreement that our schools ought to be doing better than they are at building the intellectual capabilities of American young people, it is extremely difficult to discern what really should and can be done.

The first difficulties arise with the very question of what is meant by the term "higher order skills." Many candidate definitions are available. Philosophers promote critical thinking and logical reasoning skills, developmental psychologists point to metacognition, and cognitive scientists study cognitive strategies and heuristics. Educators advocate training in study skills and problem solving. How should we make sense of these many labels? Do critical thinking, metacognition, cognitive strategies, and study skills refer to the same kinds of capabilities? And how are they related to the problem-solving abilities that mathematicians, scientists, and engineers try to teach their students? Are intelligence tests and scholastic aptitude tests good indicators of higher order skills, and if so, should we be teaching students the kinds of things that appear on these tests? What about artistic creativity and interpretive skill, and the ability to find and refine problems as well as to solve those others have set? And, perhaps most troubling of all, do any of these "intellectuals' concerns" really have much to do with what the vast majority of students will do in their work and personal lives after school? Do the higher order skills needed on the job or in the exercise of one's rights and duties as a citizen really depend on the kinds of abilities educators and the academic community are discussing?

Mingled with the difficulty of defining higher order skills is the troubling sense that there may, in fact, be little new to say about the topic. Inevitably, we hear the question: Is there really anything new about schools' trying to teach higher order skills? Haven't schools always hoped to teach students to think critically, to reason, to solve problems, to interpret, to refine ideas and to apply them in creative ways? Most of us can remember a teacher who inspired us personally in these directions, and schools everywhere include such aspirations in their statements of goals. Nevertheless, we seem to agree that students do not adequately learn these higher order abilities. Perhaps the fact that our schools have been less than successful at meeting these goals means that we have simply given up the old truths in education. Perhaps if we went back to old-fashioned courses and old-fashioned methods, the problem of teaching higher order skills would be solved without further special attention. Or, more pessimistically, perhaps we should conclude that decades of trying unsuccessfully to teach higher order skills in school show that such goals are not reachable; perhaps higher order abilities develop elsewhere than in school, and it would be wisest for schools to concentrate on the "basics," letting higher order abilities emerge later or under other auspices. To consider these fundamental questions, we need a working definition of higher order skills and an understanding of their historical role in American schools.

HIGHER ORDER SKILLS: A WORKING DEFINITION AND A HISTORICAL PERSPECTIVE

Thinking skills resist the precise forms of definition we have come to associate with the setting of specified objectives for schooling. Nevertheless, it is relatively easy to list some key features of higher order thinking. When we do this, we become aware that, although we cannot define it exactly, we can recognize higher order thinking when it occurs. Consider the following:

- Higher order thinking is *nonalgorithmic.* That is, the path of action is not fully specified in advance.
- Higher order thinking tends to be *complex.* The total path is not "visible" (mentally speaking) from any single vantage point.
- Higher order thinking often yields *multiple solutions,* each with costs and benefits, rather than unique solutions.
- Higher order thinking involves *nuanced judgment* and interpretation.
- Higher order thinking involves the application of *multiple criteria,* which sometimes conflict with one another.
- Higher order thinking often involves *uncertainty.* Not everything that bears on the task at hand is known.
- Higher order thinking involves *self-regulation* of the thinking process. We do not recognize higher order thinking in an individual when someone else "calls the plays" at every step.
- Higher order thinking involves *imposing meaning,* finding structure in apparent disorder.
- Higher order thinking is *effortful.* There is considerable mental work involved in the kinds of elaborations and judgments required.

This broad characterization of higher order thinking points to a historical fact that is often overlooked when considering the school curriculum, a fact that helps to resolve the question of what is new about our current concerns. American schools, like public schools in other industrialized countries, have inherited two quite distinct educational traditions—one concerned with elite education, the other concerned with mass education. These traditions conceived of schooling differently, had different clienteles, and held different goals for their students. Only in the last sixty years or so have the two traditions merged, at least to the extent that most students now attend comprehensive schools in which several educational programs and student groups coexist. Yet a case can be made that the continuing and as yet unresolved tension between the goals and methods of elite and mass education produces our current concern regarding the teaching of higher order skills.

If we examine the educational institutions aimed at the elite in the population, today's higher order goals are nothing new. They represent what might be called the "high literacy" strand in the history of education (Resnick and Resnick, 1977). Since there have been books and writing, there also have been schools and related institutions established to train an intellectual elite, drawn largely from privileged social strata, in capabilities of reasoning, rhetoric, mathematical and scientific thought, and other skills that today carry the higher order label. These were state, private, and religious institutions with, over the centuries, extremely varied ideas of how to go about the educational task. All were highly selective institutions. A minority of the population attended them, and this minority was selected at least in part on the basis of a taste for academic learning and the ability to perform well in a very special kind of institution.

In America, various "academies," some private and some public, carried on this tradition through the nineteenth century and into the twentieth. Until they began to be transformed early in this century, even public high schools were in the academy mold. Only a minority of young people attended or even thought of attending them. There were entrance examinations. The curriculum was quite strictly academic. Extensive writing, textual criticism, and the like were expected. Although today we might not recognize nineteenth-century academy curricula as promoting creative thinking or independent problem solving, the elite academies expected to produce, and to a considerable extent succeeded in producing, intellectual performance beyond the ordinary.

Historically, it must be stressed, the academies did not treat education of the full population of young people as within their purview. Schools for the masses arose from different roots and are a much more recent phenomenon in the history of education. Mass education derives from a "low literacy" tradition (Resnick and Resnick, 1977) aimed at producing minimal levels of competence in the general population. It originated in Europe in Reformation and counter-Reformation efforts to produce a literate, catechism- and bible-reading population. During the nineteenth century, mass schooling was adopted as part of a new national agenda in countries that were just beginning to form citizen armies and to impose common language and culture on their populations. In the United States, village and township schools were established early, probably reflecting radical Protestant traditions as well as new definitions of citizenship appropriate to the new nation. Throughout the nineteenth century, this nation knew levels of school attendance and literacy ahead of most other countries, despite the continuing flow of poor and poorly educated immigrants. As cities began to grow, massive urban school systems grew as well. Only racial minorities were systematically excluded or separated within the schools.

The mass education system that evolved under these circumstances focused largely on elementary schooling, and rather sharp divisions between elementary and secondary education persisted. This distinction was apparent both in who went to school and in what was taught. Almost everyone went to elementary school, although a limited number finished the entire eight-year course. Only a few went to high school or its equivalent. The elementary schools served the masses and concerned themselves with basic skills of reading and computation, with health and citizenship training, and the like. Routinized performance rather than creative and independent thought was stressed. Mass education was, from its inception, concerned with inculcating routine abilities: simple computation, reading predictable texts, reciting religious or civic codes. It did not take as goals for its students the ability to interpret unfamiliar texts, create material others would want and need to read, construct convincing arguments, develop original solutions to technical or social problems. The political conditions under which mass education developed encouraged instead the routinization of basic skills as well as the standardization of teaching and education institutions. Standardization was a means of ensuring that at least minimal curriculum standards would be met, that teachers would be hired on the basis of competency for the job rather than political or familial affiliation, and that those responsible for the expenditure of public funds could exercise orderly oversight over the educational process. Standardized testing was one of the methods developed to exercise oversight and centralized control of the schools (Resnick, 1980).

Early in the twentieth century, the institutional division between routine-oriented elementary schools and secondary academies in the high literacy tradition began to dissolve. Responding to changing economic and social conditions, more and more young people began to seek high school education, and educators gradually began to treat secondary education of a much larger and more varied population as being their proper concern. The secondary schools were over the next decades to become the mass institutions the elementary schools had been. The growth of this new secondary school population marked the beginning of a debate that continues even today. This debate concerns what the appropriate curriculum ought to be for secondary schools designed to serve everyone. The terms of the debate were set, in great part, by a National Education Association (NEA) commission report entitled *The Cardinal Principles of Secondary Education* (Bureau of Education, 1918). The report provided a theory and ideology for the place of a vocationally oriented curriculum in the high school as part of a diversified secondary program adapted to different types of students. This represented a clear challenge to the older ideology that organized the high school curriculum around a common core of the traditional liberal disciplines.

The tension between vocationalism and traditional disciplines as the center of the high school program has never been resolved. Responding to post-World War II manpower needs, the 1950s and early 1960s saw a greater emphasis on traditional disciplines, especially mathematics and science. Yet political and social pressures from many quarters sustained the demand for vocational training and other programs designed to keep students in school as long as possible. Other developments in the later 1960s and 1970s led to a near-complete abandonment of the traditional core curriculum, even for students who had been its traditional consumers. Schools continued to require academic courses, but the requirements were often minimal and course content focused increasingly on application and practical topics—often replacing more traditional, demanding material. Written composition and other activities that engaged higher order skills all but disappeared from the curriculum.

The effect of all of this has been to reduce, and sometimes to drive out of existence, the high literacy goals that had been the focus of the academies and their preparatory institutions. Yet the taste for such goals has survived and can be seen in recent efforts to revive interest in higher order skills teaching. This revival, however, takes place in an educational and social context that dictates an extension of high literacy goals to a much broader segment of the population than has ever before been considered capable of such learning. Today, we are committed to educating all Americans in the secondary schools and a large proportion (higher than in any other country in the world) in some form of postsecondary institution. These students' educational needs cannot be met by traditional vocational programs that no longer prepare students for productive participation in an increasingly diversified economic environment. Employers today complain that they cannot count on schools and colleges to produce young people who can move easily into more complex kinds of work. They seem to be seeking general skills such as the ability to write and speak effectively, the ability to learn easily on the job, the ability to use quantitative skills needed to apply various tools of production and management, the ability to read complex material, and the ability to build and evaluate arguments. These abilities go well beyond the routinized skills of the old mass curriculum. In fact, they are much like the abilities demanded for college-bound students in the College Board's book, *Academic Preparation for College* (College Entrance Examination Board, 1983). Yet teaching such competencies to the mass of students remains a considerable challenge.

This, then, is part of what is new about the current drive for teaching higher order skills. The goals of increasing thinking and reasoning ability are old ones for educators. Such abilities have been the goals of some schools at least since the time of Plato. But these goals were part of the high literacy tradition; they did not, by and large, apply to the more recent schools for the masses. Although it is not new to include thinking, problem solving, and reasoning in *someone's* school curriculum, it is new to include it in *everyone's* curriculum. It is new to take seriously the aspiration of making thinking and problem solving a regular part of a school program for all of the population, even minorities, even non-English speakers, even the poor. It is a new challenge to develop educational programs that assume that all individuals, not just an elite, can become competent thinkers.

THE NATURE OF THINKING AND LEARNING: GOING BEYOND THE ROUTINE

This challenge comes at a time when we also have new knowledge about the nature of thinking and strong hints about how thinking abilities are learned. In the last decade or two, cognitive science research has allowed us to look into the thinking mind, figuratively at least, and to specify more precisely the reasoning processes of both successful and less successful thinkers (Newell and Estes, 1983). More recently, researchers have begun to investigate how the ability and the propensity to think well are acquired and maintained. These two bodies of research—on the nature of human thinking and on the acquisition of thinking and learning skills—are beginning to make explicit what we mean by higher order skills and what means of cultivating such skills are most likely to be successful. This process of making explicit the abilities formerly left to the intuitions of gifted learners and teachers is precisely what we need to establish a scientific foundation for the new agenda of extending thinking and reasoning abilities to all segments of the population.

The most important single message of modern research on the nature of thinking is that the kinds of activities traditionally associated with thinking are not limited to advanced levels of development. Instead, these activities are an intimate part of even elementary levels of reading, mathematics, and other branches of learning—when learning is proceeding well. In fact, the term "higher order" skills is probably itself fundamentally misleading, for it suggests that another set of skills, presumably called "lower order," needs to come first. This assumption—that there is a sequence from lower level activities that do not require much independent thinking or judgment to higher level ones that do—colors much educational theory and practice. Implicitly at least, it justifies long years of drill on the "basics" before thinking and problem solving are demanded. Cognitive research on the nature of basic skills such as reading and mathematics provides a fundamental challenge to this assumption. Indeed, research suggests that failure to cultivate aspects of thinking such as those listed in our working definition of higher order skills may be the source of major learning difficulties even in elementary school.

Reading as a Higher Order Skill

The process of understanding a written text, as it emerges in current psychological and artificial intelligence accounts, is one in which a reader uses a combination of what is written, what he or she already knows, and various general processes (e.g., making inferences, noting connections, checking and organizing) to construct a plausible representation of what the author presumably had in mind (e.g., Just and Carpenter, 1980; Perfetti, 1985; vanDijk and Kintsch, 1983). The mental representation constructed by the reader does not match the text itself, nor does the reader even try to match it, except under special circumstances. Instead, the reader tries to represent the situation the author had in mind or the argument the author hoped to build. The reader's representation omits details that do not seem central to the message. It also *adds* information needed to make the message coherent and sensible. The written text, then, is a vehicle that permits a partially common representation of some situation or argument to be constructed by two separate minds—the writer's and the reader's.

By their nature, normal, well-written texts are incomplete expressions of the author's mental representation. They leave out some things essential to the representation on the assumption that readers will fill them in. If this assumption is not met, comprehension fails—even if every word and every sentence has been individually understood. Usually, this process of filling in is so automatic that skilled readers are quite unaware they are doing it. Only when the flow of comprehension breaks down do competent readers become aware of their inferential and interpretive processes. Yet our models of skilled comprehension suggest that inferences are being drawn and interpretations are being made throughout. And studies of eye movements during silent reading, of pause patterns as texts are read aloud, and of disruptions in comprehension caused by minor modifications at key points in the text provide convincing evidence of the reader's inferential work even for quite simple texts.

Four kinds of knowledge are called upon as readers construct meanings for texts. The first is linguistic knowledge: knowledge about how sentences are formed, rules of forward and backward reference, and the like. This knowledge is often only implicit, but readers depend on it to find common referents, to link agent to action to object, and to otherwise construct a representation of a coherent set of events and relationships. The second kind of knowledge is topical knowledge, that is, knowledge about the text's subject matter. Like linguistic knowledge, topical knowledge is often used so automatically that readers are unaware of its contribution. Third, readers invoke knowledge about rules of inference. This knowledge, too, is likely to be implicit for the skilled reader. Finally, knowledge of conventional rhetorical structures often aids the process of text interpretation.

An example drawn from the work of Walter Kintsch (1979) demonstrates the role of the first three kinds of knowledge in reading comprehension and shows how interactive they are:

> The Swazi tribe was at war with a neighboring tribe because of a dispute over some cattle. Among the warriors were two unmarried men named Kakra and his younger brother Gum. Kakra was killed in battle. According to tribal custom, Kakra was married subsequently to the woman Ami.

The first three sentences of this short passage are understood so effortlessly that the reader does not notice the special linguistic work required to build a coherent representation. Yet some inference is required. Note that the term "warriors" in the second sentence has not appeared before. However, the definite article "the" that precedes the term implies that warriors have been referred to previously. The skilled individual knows this linguistic rule, even if only implicitly. What is more, such a reader *infers* the required referent by using topical knowledge: namely, that a war (which *is* referred to in the preceding sentence) is likely to involve warriors.

Greater difficulty is encountered when the fourth sentence is reached. The sentence is puzzling. It seems anomalous, and even contradictory, in the context of the preceding sentences. To know that the final sentence is anomalous, the reader must bring topical knowledge and rules of inference to bear. The reader knows, for example, that someone killed in battle is no longer alive. In addition, he or she is likely to assume that marriage requires a living bridegroom. This leads to the inference that it is impossible for Kakra to be married after the battle. Topical knowledge and rules of inference thus lead to the sense that the passage is incomprehensible. Yet topical knowledge can also provide the basis for resolving the comprehension problem. The knowledge needed relates to ghost marriage, a tribal custom in which, when the oldest son of a family dies without heirs, his spirit is nevertheless married as planned, and his younger brother takes his place in the marriage bed until an heir is produced.

In longer texts, knowledge about rhetorical structures also interacts with linguistic, topical, and inference rule knowledge. Narrative stories, for example, frequently conform to a prototypical structure in which, after a setting is described, an initiating event sets up a situation in which a character responds by setting a goal. In successive episodes the character attempts to attain the goal, each attempt producing an outcome and a response to the outcome. Extensive research on story "grammars" (see Stein and Trabasso, 1982) has shown that people depend on this prototypical structure to understand and interpret stories. Readers are sensitive to the order in which categories of information are presented. They have difficulty recalling stories when information is given in an order other than that specified in the idealized story schema, and—most important as evidence that this story schema plays a key role in understanding— people tend to recall story information in the order predicted by the schema even if the version of the story they read or heard uses a nonstandard order. Expository texts, too, follow certain standard rhetorical forms. Structures such as compare/contrast, cause/effect, or problem/solution provide frameworks that support and sustain communication between author and reader. When an author uses a familiar text structure, it serves as a kind of scaffolding for the reader's interpretive work. For example, structural markers like "on the other hand" and "furthermore" are used to signal rhetorical functions.

This broad analysis of comprehension as a meaning-imposing process that depends on the reader's knowledge of text structure as well as linguistic, topical, and inferential knowledge is common to all current cognitive theories of reading. Furthermore, when studies compare successful and less successful readers, the former always turn out both to possess more of these kinds of knowledge and to be more likely to use that knowledge spontaneously. Although there are important differences among theories with respect to specific aspects of these processes—their timing, the kinds of cues that set them in motion, the ways in which knowledge is organized—there are no disagreements regarding the general characterization of comprehension.

Research still does not provide a clear answer about the extent to which meaning imposition proceeds strategically, in a deliberate, self-conscious fashion rather than automatically and unconsciously. Much evidence suggests that, for a skilled reader not totally new to the text's topic, most of the work to build a text representation proceeds quite unconsciously through processes of automatic activation. The process slows down, requires deliberate attention, and becomes accessible to conscious awareness under special conditions: when there is an anomaly in the text or some unusual linguistic construction; when the topical domain is so unfamiliar that the reader lacks necessary prior knowledge for interpretation; when a particularly complicated chain of reasoning is presented; or when the reader wants to study and remember the text rather than just understand it (see chapters in Mandl et al., 1984, for a discussion of many of these issues). Some psychologists (e.g., Collins and Smith, 1982) believe that the same processes of self-questioning, summarizing, and the like go on in highly skilled reading as in more self-conscious reading, but at a much faster rate. Other research (e.g., Neves and Anderson, 1981; Newell and Rosenbloom, 1981) suggests that as readers develop automatic skills the nature of the process actually changes and certain steps drop out. In any case, it is evident that educators ought to aim to produce both kinds of reading comprehension abilities among students: the ability to understand written texts automatically and with little effort, and the capacity to apply deliberate strategies for interpreting and remembering when the need arises.

It is striking that the processes identified in cognitive research on

reading comprehension are related to the techniques of textual exege-
sis and analysis commonly taught in high-level courses in literature,
philosophy, and other disciplines in which multiple interpretations of
texts are discussed as part of instruction. Cognitive theory, in other
words, suggests that processes traditionally reserved for advanced
students—that is, for a minority who have developed skill and taste
for interpretive mental work—might be taught to all readers, including young children and, perhaps especially, those who learn with
difficulty. Cognitive research suggests that these processes *are what
we mean by reading comprehension.* Not to teach them is to ignore
the most important aspects of reading. This convergence of cognitive research on reading with traditional high literacy concerns offers
some promise that the goal of extending high literacy standards to
the mass educational system can be achieved.

Meaning Construction in Mathematics

A higher order interpretation of the basic mathematics curriculum is less straightforward than we have been able to propose for
reading. Nevertheless, a close consideration of recent research on
mathematical cognition suggests that in mathematics, as in reading,
successful learners understand the task to be one of *constructing
meaning,* of doing interpretive work rather than routine manipu-
lations. In mathematics, the problem of imposing meaning takes a
special form: making sense of formal symbols and rules that are often
taught as if they were arbitrary conventions rather than expressions
of fundamental regularities and relationships among quantities and
physical entities.

Recent research on mathematics learning points to an apparent
paradox. We have abundant evidence that young children—even
before attending school—develop rather robust, although simple,
mathematical concepts and that they are able to apply these concepts in a variety of practical situations. Yet school mathematics is
decidedly difficult to learn for many children. Children's first and
best-developed mathematical competence is counting (Gelman and
Gallistel, 1978). Several investigations have shown that young children are able to use counting to solve informally a wide variety of
arithmetic problems, including problems that they have difficulty
solving in school (Carraher et al., 1985; Ginsburg, 1977). Furthermore, an examination of shortcut procedures invented by children

suggests an implicit understanding of several basic arithmetic principles. For example, the *min* procedure (first documented by Groen and Parkman, 1972) is an addition strategy that involves setting a mental "counter" at the larger of the two addends, regardless of whether it is the first or second, and then incrementing by the smaller. The child's use of such a procedure requires acknowledgment, at least implicitly, of the commutativity principle of addition. Several studies (e.g., Svenson and Hedenborg, 1979; Woods et al., 1975) have shown that children, starting at about age seven, solve subtraction problems by either counting down from the larger number or counting up from the smaller number, whichever will require the fewest counts. This procedure reveals implicit knowledge of the complementarity of addition and subtraction, which in turn depends on thinking of the minuend (top number) as a whole, with a decomposition into the subtrahend and the difference. These examples and many others suggest that an intuitive understanding of many basic mathematical principles develops early and finds expression in various kinds of practical problem-solving tasks.

There is substantial evidence that children's difficulty in learning school mathematics derives in large part from their failure to recognize and apply the relations between formal rules taught in school and their own independently developed mathematical intuitions. Part of the evidence lies in close analysis of the kinds of errors that children typically make in the course of learning arithmetic and, eventually, algebra. To an important degree, calculation errors derive not from random or careless "slips" but from systematically applying incorrect procedures. These incorrect rules, of course, are not taught. Children invent them, as they do the shortcut strategies. By analyzing their incorrect rules we can understand what children are and are not attending to as they learn arithmetic. The most carefully studied domain of arithmetic errors is subtraction. The kinds of errors (called "bugs" from their similarity to minicomputer programs with bugs in them) that children make have been carefully documented; these bugs serve as the basis for an artificial intelligence program (Brown and Van Lehn, 1980) that invents the same subtraction bugs children invent but does not invent the many other logically possible bugs not observed in children. Because the program's performance largely matches children's performance, its processes and knowledge base provide a theory of what children probably know and do that leads them to buggy inventions.

According to the Brown and Van Lehn theory, children invent

buggy procedures when they encounter problems for which they have no complete algorithm available. This may occur because they have not yet been taught what to do in special cases (for example, how does one borrow from a zero?) or because they have forgotten certain steps in procedures already taught. To respond, children engage in a form of problem solving: generating possible actions and testing them against a list of constraints. Although this is an intelligent problem-solving process, it produces errors because certain key constraints are missing from the test list. The missing constraints have to do with the *meaning* of the symbols; constraints regarding how the symbols ought to *look* on the page (e.g., only one digit per column, borrow marks in appropriate places) are largely obeyed. What is more, the program has no representation at all of the quantities that are involved; it only has rules for manipulating symbols. This suggests that children, like the program, solve arithmetic problems by manipulating symbols while ignoring their meaning (Resnick, 1987).

We can reach the same conclusion from an analysis of the characteristic errors made by students learning decimal fractions (Hiebert and Wearne, 1985) and algebra (Matz, 1982; Resnick et al., 1987; Sleeman, 1983). Research on algebra learning shows that when thinking about transformation rules, students rarely refer either to quantitative relationships or to problem situations that could give meaning to algebra expressions. Not surprisingly, students are not very skillful at the process of "mathematizing," that is, at constructing links between formal algebraic expressions and the actual situations to which they refer (e.g., Clement, 1982). All of this points to a conclusion that current mathematics education does not adequately engage students' interpretive and meaning-construction capacities. This conclusion is supported by data from national assessments (e.g., National Assessment of Educational Progress, 1983) showing declines in students' mathematics problem-solving skills even as calculation abilities rise. In short, most students learn mathematics as a routine skill; they do not develop higher order capacities for organizing and interpreting information.

It seems likely that a less routinized approach to mathematics could produce substantial improvements in learning. Although the evidence is limited, it suggests that successful math learners engage in more metacognitive behaviors (e.g., checking their own understanding of procedures, monitoring for consistency, trying to relate new material to prior knowledge) during math learning; they are also less likely to practice symbol manipulation rules without reference to the meaning of the symbols (Peterson et al., 1984; Resnick, 1987). Strong math learners also engage in more task analysis (Dweck, in press); that is, they figure out alternative strategies for attacking problems and generating solvable subproblems. These sense-making and knowledge-extending activities parallel those that are so well documented for high levels of reading skill. They are also activities generally viewed as characteristic of high levels of mathematics thinking and problem solving. Thus, we again see a convergence between the processes identified by cognitive research and those associated with traditional elite mathematics education.

GENERAL REASONING: IMPROVING INTELLIGENCE

Mathematics and reading are not unique in the extent to which high-level performance depends on processes of monitoring one's understanding, imposing meaning and structure, and raising questions about presented material. Much the same story can be told about all the subject matter in the school curriculum and about all but the most routine job performances. Recent research in science problem solving, for example, shows that experts do not respond to problems as they are presented—writing equations for every relationship described and then using routine procedures for manipulating equations. Instead, they reinterpret the problems, recasting them in terms of general scientific principles until the solutions become almost self-evident (Larkin et al., 1980). Expert writers treat the process of composing an essay as a complex task of shaping a communication that will appeal to and convince an intended audience rather than as a simple task of writing down everything they know about a topic (Bereiter and Scardamalia, 1982; Flower and Hayes, 1980). In the social sciences, trained thinkers call upon a wide range of knowledge relevant to a topic to construct proposals for action and to build justifications for those proposals that conform to many of the classical principles of rhetorical argumentation (Voss et al., 1983). Skilled technicians repairing equipment do not just proceed through routine checklists; instead, they construct "mental models" of complex systems and use these to reason about possible causes of observed breakdowns and potential repairs (e.g., de Kleer and Brown, 1980).

In all of these cases, certain kinds of higher order thinking recur: experts elaborate and reconstruct problems into new forms; they look for consistencies and inconsistencies in proposed solutions; they pursue implications of initial ideas and make modifications rather than seeking quick solutions and sticking with initial ideas; they reason by analogy to other, similar situations. These similarities, long noted in discussions of intelligence (see Journal of Educational Psychology, 1921; Simon, 1976; Sternberg and Detterman, 1979) and problem solving (Tuma and Reif, 1980), lead naturally to the question of whether there might not be some general thinking skills that would produce improved ability to learn across many traditional curriculum areas. If such skills exist and if we can find effective ways to teach them, we can imagine an important increase in educational efficiency, for—it would seem—a relatively narrow instructional effort might produce wide learning results.

The search for general learning skills is not a new one. both educators and psychologists have long sought to identify and to characterize such skills, the former because of the educational efficiency such skills could help them realize, the latter in search of unifying characteristics of human thought. Psychological research gives us reason to believe in the reality of general skills for learning as well as reason to maintain a degree of skepticism. In the next section we will review recent efforts to teach higher order skills. These efforts provide the newest body of evidence on the question of whether such skills are teachable. Before proceeding to that review, however, we should first consider what the body of past research would suggest.

Past Research

Psychometric research provides the best-established evidence for the existence of cognitive skills that play a role in diverse kinds of learning. When two or more cognitive abilities are tested, there is almost always a positive correlation between the measures. People who do well on one ability test are, on the average, likely to do well on the others. Virtually the only conditions under which such a correlation is not found are those in which tests have been specifically designed not to correlate. For example, investigators have built tests of creativity explicitly designed to be psychometrically independent of IQ. Tests that correlate positively are presumed to share underlying processes. The fact that most intelligence tests do correlate strongly and that a general factor can always be identified through statistical methods such as factor analysis suggests that all tests have some processes in common. These common processes are, presumably, general abilities.

Of course, such findings only raise new questions. How do we characterize these common processes? Is there reason to think they are teachable? When cognitive scientists do information-processing analyses of complex skills, they find the same kinds of basic problem-solving processes used in task after task (Simon, 1976). For example, one of the earliest uses of computers to explore processes of human reasoning resulted in the construction of a program that solved symbolic logic problems. This program was called the General Problem Solver (GPS) in the belief that its processes would play a role in solving many kinds of problems, not just those of symbolic logic. This has turned out to be partly true. Although GPS itself can solve only a limited range of problems, the kinds of processes used by GPS appear over and over again in simulations of human performance of complex tasks. Processes such as means–ends analysis (comparing one's final goal with results that would be produced by procedures currently available), subgoal formation (forming a new goal that is easier to solve and that is en route to the final goal), generate-and-test routines (generating actions and testing them against constraints), and other general problem-solving routines are used in tasks as varied as inventing buggy arithmetic routines, planning compositions, constructing geometry proofs, and troubleshooting electronic devices. The reason that a single artificial intelligence program cannot solve a wide variety of problems is not that the fundamental processes it applies are widely different across domains, but rather that the program must apply these processes to very specific, organized bodies of knowledge. Each simulation must build in the relevant knowledge, and so it becomes specific to its knowledge base (see Dehn and Schank, 1982).

Other processes that appear repeatedly in analyses of complex task performance play a kind of "executive" or self-regulatory role in thinking. People use these processes to keep track of their own understanding, to initiate review or rehearsal activities when needed, and to deliberately organize their attention and other resources in order to learn something. These activities have been shown to be characteristic of effective learners, good readers and writers, and strong problem solvers. The same processes are relatively absent in younger or less intelligent individuals. These skills are sometimes called "metacognitive skills" (see Brown et al., 1983) because they operate on an individual's own cognitive processes. They have been suggested frequently as processes that could be taught and that would enhance learning and thinking in a wide range of specific situations.

The problem-solving skills identified in cognitive simulation research and the metacognitive skills identified in developmental psychology research have both been proposed as candidates for teaching. The hope is held out that if we can improve specific skills through some form of direct teaching, then people's ability to perform various kinds of learning, thinking, and problem-solving tasks in which such skills have been observed will also improve.

On the other hand, the very body of research that has helped to identify the candidate "general" skills also provides reason for questioning their educational importance. Cognitive research yields repeated demonstrations that specific content area knowledge plays a central role in reasoning, thinking, and learning of all kinds. I have already alluded to several examples of the importance of specific knowledge. Specific knowledge about a text's topic affects processes of language comprehension, for example. Skilled science problem solvers rely on their knowledge of scientific principles to recast problems into more elegant and easily solvable forms. Political scientists' argumentation becomes degraded when they know little about the particular problem or the particular part of the world under discussion (Voss et al., 1983). Even on the tasks used to assess general intelligence or scholastic aptitude, recent analyses have made it clear that much depends on specific knowledge: of vocabulary, of particular number relationships, of possible transformations of visual displays, and the like (cf. Glaser, 1984). General skills such as breaking down a problem into simpler problems or checking to see whether one has captured the main idea of a passage may be impossible to apply if one does not have a store of knowledge about similar problems—or know enough about the topic to be able to recognize its central ideas. Of course, to appreciate the dependence of general skills application on specific knowledge is not to deny that such general skills exist. Yet such an understanding raises questions about the wisdom of attempting to develop thinking skills outside the context of specific knowledge domains. It suggests that a more promising route may be to teach thinking skills within specific disciplines and perhaps hope for some transfer to other disciplines as relevant knowledge is acquired.

On first consideration the hope for transfer of thinking abilities across disciplines seems misplaced. A long history of research exists on transfer among school subjects. Over the decades, educators have espoused a recurring belief that certain school subject matters "discipline the mind" and therefore should be taught not so much for their inherent value as for their efficacy in facilitating other learning. Latin was defended for many years in these terms; mathematics and logic are often so defended today. Most recently, computer programming has been proposed as a way to develop general problem-solving and reasoning abilities (e.g., Papert, 1980). The view that we can expect strong transfer from learning in one area to improvements across the board has never been well supported empirically. At the turn of the century, Thorndike and Woodworth (1901) studied transfer among school subjects and found that it was more efficient to study the subject of interest (English vocabulary, for example) than to study some other subject (e.g., Latin) that "prepared" one's mind. Subsequent reviews of research on transfer of school subject matter generally have reconfirmed Thorndike and Woodworth's finding.

Nevertheless, the history of transfer research need not be totally discouraging; most of this research does not directly address the questions of most concern to those whose goal is the improvement of general thinking and learning abilities. First, the subject matter teaching in these studies has rarely been aimed at developing transferable skill and knowledge. We thus do not know what leverage there might be in instruction explicitly aimed at producing general skills in the context of a particular discipline. Second, evaluations of learning outcomes have rested mainly on what *knowledge* was acquired in the transfer discipline, rather than on whether skills for *acquiring* knowledge in that discipline have been enhanced. The issue of transferability of thinking and learning skills, then, is still open.

Current Programs for Teaching Higher Order Skills

Recently, a variety of courses and programs claiming to teach reasoning and problem-solving abilities have emerged (see Nickerson et al., 1985; Segal et al., 1985). These represent the newest wave of optimism concerning the teachability of general higher order cognitive skills. Some programs focus on problem solving and reasoning in particular disciplines. But most are aimed at enhancing general skills or at using a combination of both approaches. Recent programs thus offer an opportunity to update the empirical record concerning the effects of various kinds of training in thinking and reasoning skills. In the course of this study, nominations have been sought of programs aimed at teaching various aspects of higher order thinking.

A large number of programs and reports have been examined. They are discussed here in several broad categories.

Problem Solving in the Disciplines

Faculty members in a number of disciplines have developed courses or course-adjuncts designed to improve the problem-solving ability of students in their disciplines. These are generally college-level programs aimed at the full range of students in the discipline. The majority of such courses have been developed in the physical sciences (e.g., Reif and St. John, 1979), engineering (e.g., Fuller, 1978; Rubinstein, 1980; Woods, 1983; Woods et al., 1984), and mathematics (e.g., Schoenfeld, 1982, 1983, 1985). Wales and Stager (1977; see also Wales and Nardi, 1985) have proposed a general strategy, which they call "Guided Design," for teaching problem solving and decision making within the context of a variety of subject matters. Guided Design courses have been offered in high schools as well as colleges and in the humanities and social sciences as well as in the physical sciences and engineering.

Problem-solving courses and programs vary considerably in scope and in style, ranging from individual courses or laboratory programs to a multicourse sequence spread over several years of college. The reported programs are probably representative of similar programs being used on many campuses that have not been formally described. Some of the programs are highly structured, with printed materials, special lab notebooks, standard exercises, and regular evaluations. Others are essentially suggestions to instructors, including guidance in how to conduct classroom discussions to favor the development of problem-solving skills.

Central to all programs is extensive practice in solving problems or in designing and carrying out experiments. Supportive help is offered, and problem complexity gradually increases. Some programs also teach students to use particular heuristic strategies including special forms of problem representation. For example, Fuller's chemical engineering course requires students to prepare special graphical representations (Polya maps) that show a problem's structure. Reif's laboratory requires lab reports in which students organize hierarchically the important aspects of an experiment.

Various forms of social interaction are used, both to make visible normally covert aspects of the problem-solving process and to increase students' self-conscious monitoring and management of their thought processes. These include having the instructor think aloud while solving problems set by students, having students work in pairs or larger teams, and having students justify solutions to one another and evaluate each other's solutions. Particular attention is often paid to the uncertainties of problem solving and to the process of making and correcting—rather than avoiding or denying—errors.

Formal evaluation of problem-solving programs is rare. The most extensive quantitative evaluation data are presented by Wales (1979) for freshmen for the first six years of the Guided Design program in engineering at West Virginia University. Wales found definite rises in both freshman and four-year grade point averages (GPAs) even after controlling for grade inflation that occurred during the study period. Before the introduction of Guided Design, engineering students' average freshman GPAs were below the university average; after Guided Design, their GPAs were well above the average. Students who had participated in the Guided Design program as freshmen also had higher four-year GPAs than (transfer) students who had not participated. During the same period, entering students' ACT (American College Testing Program Assessment) scores remained roughly constant. The percentage of students completing the four-year course also increases; thus, the grade increase cannot be attributed to a more selective university policy. Other Guided Design users have reported similar results.

Other problem-solving programs have not reported this kind of extensive quantitative data, but several document favorable student evaluations of their programs and describe examples of improved problem solving displayed by individual students (e.g., Fuller, 1975; Reif and St. John, 1979; Woods et al., 1984). In general, most program authors cited here can point to long-term use of their courses on their campuses, attesting to both faculty and student enthusiasm. Further, because these programs are designed, by and large, to teach skills that are directly desired in their disciplines, the question of transfer is not as relevant as for some of the other programs to be discussed. Nevertheless, more attention to evaluation issues—and especially the use of more informative measures than overall grade averages—would strengthen the case for these types of courses.

General Problem-Solving Skills

Another group of programs aims to teach general problem-solving abilities that will be applicable in many different settings.

The CoRT Thinking Program (de Bono, 1976, 1985) and the Productive Thinking Program (Covington, 1985, in press) represent two visible and useful examples of this kind of program.

CoRT grows out of a tradition of training executives and designers to increase fluency and creativity in practical problem solving (see de Bono, 1970). A version of the program suitable for schoolchildren recently has been produced and commercially marketed. It is probably the most widely used thinking skills program, having been translated into several languages and officially adopted for school use in several countries. CoRT focuses on mastering a set of "attention-directing" tools that, when applied, lead one to consider multiple sides of an issue, to consider consequences, to select objectives and weigh factors involved in a situation, to generate and evaluate evidence, and the like. Lessons are as content-free as possible—that is, they use familiar situations and very short presentations to establish contexts in which the tools can be used. A great premium is placed on quick use of taught strategies and on the number and variety of ideas generated. De Bono refers to this as perceptual rather than logical thinking and is more concerned with effective "real-life" thinking than with improving school performance.

The Productive Thinking Program was designed specifically for upper elementary schoolchildren. It, too, teaches a variety of strategies for planning, managing, and monitoring one's own thinking. Although stated in quite different language and embedded in more complex (though still nonacademic) problem settings, the strategies taught appear similar in intent to those of the CoRT program. Both programs seem to teach versions of the planning and metacognitive strategies that have been identified in information-processing research on problem solving (cf. Polson and Jeffries, 1985) along with the kind of fluency in idea generation associated with certain definitions of creativity. Covington's theory and program also emphasize motivation and self-concept, helping students to think of themselves as problem solvers and to resist immobilization caused by fear of failure.

The Productive Thinking Program has been evaluated quite extensively over a number of years (see Covington, in press, for the most recent reports). There is evidence that students in the program become good at generating ideas and questions and increase their use of the planning strategies in the kinds of problem situations on which training is given. Furthermore, trained students' advantages last for some months. Most important, students seem to apply the program's planning strategies (e.g., analyzing the task, outlining an action plan) to school tasks such as preparing a report or exhibit. However, the latter assessments consisted of self-reports; therefore, we do not know if students actually apply these skills in practice.

The CoRT program has been evaluated less often than its widespread adoption might suggest. Nickerson et al. (1985, pp. 217–220; see also Edwards et al., 1984) summarize several studies; these show that students taking the course tend to become substantially more fluent in producing ideas, may make some progress toward higher levels of abstraction, and may take a more balanced view of problems. Changes also often occur in students' conceptions of themselves as learners. However, these findings come from performances on problems very similar to those used in the CoRT training. The only assessments of transfer to practical or school problem solving come from students who report using the strategies in their everyday lives. Thus, judgments of CoRT's educational value must depend on the importance one attaches to the strategies directly taught and to ideational fluency as such. We do not have empirical evidence of the kind of effects these have on school learning or on success in practical problem solving, although many people feel that the CoRT program has helped them or their children in both.

Reading and Study Strategies

Perhaps the largest set of training approaches and programs is directed at teaching strategies for reading and studying from texts (e.g., Dansereau, 1985; Jones et al., 1985; Jones et al., 1984; Paris et al., 1984; Weinstein and Underwood, 1985). Programs for enhancing reading and studying skills have been developed for virtually every educational level from elementary school to the university. Some authors stress the study skill aspect of their programs; others emphasize the reading skill aspect. In fact, however, it is often difficult to distinguish between the two. Programs and research studies use different labels to describe a common set of strategies including skimming, using context to figure out words and meaning, self-testing to check one's understanding, and generating summaries as one reads. The strategies taught in these programs are all based on cognitive research in reading; they involve various kinds of elaborations the reader can make on the basis of the text. The strategies taught are those that have been observed in expert readers and in strong students but that are often found to be lacking in weaker readers. They are also strategies that accord well with theories of reading expertise and with cognitive science models of the reading process.

Some techniques are reminiscent of older study skill techniques. These include special forms of notetaking intended to highlight relations among different parts of the text's content and to help readers organize their knowledge (Dansereau, 1985; Jones et al., 1985). In some cases, the study skills and reading strategies are embedded in fairly extensive programs that also help students plan their time, manage study activities, control anxiety and mood, and apply deliberate learning strategies in typical academic study situations (e.g., Dansereau, 1985; Weinstein and Underwood, 1985).

Considerable effort has gone into quantitative evaluations of these strategy training programs. Evaluation results reveal the theoretical and practical complexities of these research efforts. Paris and his colleagues, for example, have studied carefully the effects of training elementary schoolchildren in strategies such as skimming, using context to figure out unfamiliar words, and taking notes (Paris and Jacobs, 1984; Paris et al., 1984). In a series of studies, they have shown that students became more aware of comprehension strategies and report using them more often. On the other hand, the effect of these improvements on general reading skill is slight when measured by traditional comprehension measures, which typically require answering questions about short passages. The trained children do excel in tasks that evoke deliberate attention to the structure and meaning of the text, such as detecting errors and filling in missing words. Because good performance on such tasks is known to correlate well with reading comprehension, one might expect transfer to the more commonly used passage comprehension measures. Determining why such transfer does not occur or what additional training features might produce transfer is likely to occupy investigators in the field for some time.

Weinstein has reported that her college-level study skills course has positive effects on reading performance, using a general reading test. She also documents lowered test anxiety and improvements in student-reported study habits. Dansereau has shown similar results, using more direct study measures in which students were given an hour to study 3,000-word passages and were tested a week later; these tests included essay questions as well as more standard test items. As with other programs, some evaluation problems did exist. In both program evaluations it was difficult to establish optimal control groups. Furthermore, the effect of a total study skills program, rather than the effect of a particular study strategy or teaching method, was under scrutiny. However, Dansereau has also conducted a number of separate studies of particular component strategies. This mixture of global evaluation with detailed analyses of the effects of specific component strategies, pursued in a cumulative fashion and extended so that long-term effects and transfer can be evaluated, is precisely what we need to establish which elements of complex programs are important to their overall effects.

Self-Monitoring Skills

Direct strategy training may be only partially helpful in increasing performance because many individuals primarily lack good judgment regarding when strategies should be applied. Extensive research supports this prediction. For example, research with retarded individuals shows that it is relatively easy to improve memory task performance by simply instructing people to rehearse or to engage in verbal elaboration and other mnemonic activities. Typically, the improvement comes almost immediately, suggesting that the strategies are, in some sense, already known. However, in these studies there was almost complete lack of transfer, even to tasks that were only slightly modified. This meant that retarded individuals' difficulty was in not knowing when memory strategies were called for rather than in being unable to use the strategies. Recent training studies that focused on appropriate application of strategies have shown more promising results (see Brown et al., 1983, for a review of this research).

Overuse of deliberate strategies can also be maladaptive. Reading would be neither pleasurable nor efficient if one continuously did the kinds of deliberate processing taught in the study skill experiments just described. These strategies are useful when automatic processing breaks down, but they can be very intrusive and disruptive when applied unnecessarily. The more skilled the reader, the more likely he or she will know when to apply the strategies—and when to avoid them. Weak readers tend to apply strategies indiscriminately, thus disrupting comprehension, or tend to drop them entirely when there is no longer a teacher present to insist on their use and demonstration.

Because of these observations, some investigators have suggested that readers—particularly weak readers—might profit more from developing self-monitoring skills than from practicing specific text interpretation strategies. Palincsar and Brown's (1984) work represents the most striking advance in this direction. Working with middle-school children who had extremely weak reading comprehension skills, they introduced a process of "reciprocal teaching" in which children worked cooperatively to develop an interpretation of a text. To facilitate interpretation, children took turns posing questions about and summarizing the texts. Sometimes they also made predictions about what would be said in a following section of text or asked for clarification. The teacher modeled these processes for the children in think-aloud form. Other group members commented on the quality of questions or summaries and tried to help improve them. There was no practice in *answering* questions or in any particular strategies for using context, analyzing words, or the like.

Reciprocal teaching sessions were conducted daily for several weeks. During this training period the children's skill at answering questions about passages that they read privately also began to rise. They maintained improved reading test performance even after an eight-week period without reciprocal teaching sessions. Furthermore, scores on science and social studies comprehension tests, given in the classroom rather than in the special reciprocal teaching laboratory, also rose significantly. Comparisons with groups of children who engaged in intensive reading practice without the reciprocal teaching support establish the importance of reciprocal teaching in producing these results. These levels of retention and transfer are rare in educational intervention studies. More important, accumulating evidence demonstrates that variants of reciprocal teaching can be effectively carried out by regular classroom teachers as part of their normal instruction.

Other studies focusing on self-monitoring and meaning construction skills have also shown promising although not as dramatic results as Palincsar and Brown's (e.g., Bereiter and Bird, 1985; Collins et al., 1981; Day, 1980). In all of these studies, learning proceeded in a social setting in which tutor and students shared responsibility for text interpretation. The tutor modeled certain interpretive processes; these were then taken over by students. There was some attention to building students' awareness of their own level of understanding as well. Schoenfeld (1985) has used a similar approach in teaching mathematics problem solving.

The findings on reciprocal teaching and its cousins point to a promising educational intervention. However, they also highlight how little we know about exactly how such training produces its effects. How can instruction focused on overt, self-conscious strategies that may not be actual components of skilled performance improve normally automatic processes? Some cognitive scientists believe that question asking and summarizing become automated in the course of learning and are present in skilled reading in abbreviated, fast, and therefore largely invisible form. Others suggest that these abilities are not actively invoked during the course of automatic comprehension—although they may well be used during studying and when smooth comprehension breaks down. In that case, the monitoring strategies taught and children's subsequent skilled reading performance would be only indirectly related. Perhaps practice in deliberate, mindful, or "intentional" reading activates certain powerful knowledge structures that can be applied in subsequent reading. Perhaps practice mitigates emotional difficulties associated with years of perceiving oneself as a poor reader. At present, many explanations seem possible, but the actual learning mechanisms have not been identified. Research has located a "psychological space" in which educationally powerful effects seem to occur, but it has not yet adequately explained what happens in the space to produce the effects. Until we can provide a more substantial theoretical explanation, we can probably expect mixed results from both laboratory and classroom experiments aimed at training self-monitoring skills and strategies because it will be difficult to determine in advance the essential components of a training approach.

Components of Intelligence

A number of programs aim to improve general intelligence through special training. Among the best known of these are Whimbey and Lochhead's (1982, 1984) program for high school and college students, Feuerstein's Instrumental Enrichment Program (Feuerstein et al., 1985), the Venezuela "Project Intelligence" program (Bolt Beranek and Newman, 1983), and Sternberg's (1986) program for developing practical intelligence.

The program of actually defining intelligence is addressed only indirectly by most of these program developers. Their programs provide practice and feedback on the kinds of tasks that usually appear in intelligence and aptitude tests. These include vocabulary-building activities, exercises involving synonyms and antonyms, analogies, spatial reasoning items, and certain kinds of logic tasks of a more or less puzzlelike nature. By including such tasks, the program developers implicitly accept the validity of established tests as indicators of intelligence. However, the history of the field (e.g., Journal of Educational Psychology, 1921; Sternberg and Detterman, 1979) shows that psychologists have never arrived at a fully satisfactory definition of intelligence.

Recognizing this limitation, two of the programs extend their reach substantially beyond the usual testlike tasks. Sternberg's program aims to teach problem-solving techniques drawn from cognitive research, strategies for memorizing and reading, various practical skills (e.g., interviewing and clinical reasoning), and methods for overcoming emotional blocks. The program text, intended for high school or college courses, assumes that students' performance will improve when they receive information about psychological theories. In this sense, it can be seen as the most recent in a series of self-improvement courses designed by psychologists to reflect cognitive research on thinking and problem solving (cf. Hayes, 1981; Wickelgren, 1974). The Venezuela Project Intelligence course also includes tasks that go beyond intelligence test types of exercises. These include lessons on the structure of language and the analysis of arguments that are similar to material taught in the informal logic and critical thinking programs discussed in the next section of this essay. Other lessons cover the use of graphic, tabular, and simulation representations. A range of problem-solving, decision-making, and design activities, similar to those included in programs on problem solving in the disciplines, is also included. By contrast, several programs marketed under the titles of "critical thinking," "reasoning," or "thinking skills" are actually composed mainly of testlike exercises.

Two intelligence training programs, Whimbey and Lochhead's and Feuerstein's, particularly stress social mediation in learning cognitive skills. Whimbey and Lochhead suggest that their exercises be used in a "pair problem-solving" process in which students alternate the roles of problem-solver (thinking aloud) and listener-critic. The intent, as in some of the mathematics and engineering problem-solving programs described earlier, is to make the problem-solving process overt and to give students practice in analyzing problems and working through errors rather than avoiding them. Feuerstein's Instrumental Enrichment Program is intended for functionally backward students. It tries to provide, in condensed form, the kind of help in explicitly analyzing tasks, formulating strategies, and evaluating outcomes that is provided incidentally in normal development through interaction with parents and other caretakers. In Instrumental Enrichment training, student–teacher interaction, together with specially structured group discussions following the completion of individual exercises, plays this mediating role.

Adequate program evaluation is sparse, except in the case of the Venezuela program. That program has been subjected to a fairly extensive evaluation involving experimental and control classes in the seventh grade (students aged 11–17) in *barrio* (impoverished urban district) schools. Evaluation demonstrated a clear effect of the course on a verbal IQ measure and on several general ability tests, including reading. Experimental students performed better than control students on several measures of the skills directly taught in the course. In addition, a smaller student sample also took special oral and written posttests assessing qualitative aspects of thinking such as appropriateness of a design, clarity of expression, and use of supporting reasons. Here, too, the experimental group outperformed the control.

The special posttest in the Venezuela evaluation is important because it examines transfer of the skills taught to educationally and practically relevant tasks. Researchers must establish this kind of transfer whenever teaching focuses on activities that are valued because of their association with socially valued competence, rather than valued for their own worth. This is clearly the case for IQ tests. These tests are used in evaluation studies because the tests are quite good at predicting school performance. But students trained to do well on the tests themselves will not necessarily do better in school. IQ tests probably correlate with school performance mainly because doing well on both the IQ tasks and school tasks depends on learning abilities and strategies not directly observed in either. Therefore, specialized, targeted training on IQ-like tasks may not generalize. Direct assessment of transfer is needed. Unfortunately, apart from the promising but limited evidence from the Venezuela program, such assessments have not been made. Performance on particular types of items or on IQ tests as a whole has been shown to improve with training (e.g., Feuerstein et al., 1985; Sternberg, 1986). However, evidence that improved test scores predict improved performance on problem solving or learning tasks closer to those of school or "real life" is rare (see Lochhead, 1985, for a perspicacious discussion of the difficulties of evaluations that include this kind of transfer criterion).

Informal Logic and Critical Thinking

The final approach to the teaching of higher order skills to be considered here emerges from a philosophical rather than a psychological tradition. In the past several years philosophers at a number of universities have turned their attention to problems of teaching general reasoning and argumentation skills. Their work is rooted in ancient traditions of rhetoric and in recent work on the logic of argumentation (see, e.g., Toulmin et al., 1979). The current focus on the analysis of extended discourse on complex topics, usually social issues, represents a new thrust within philosophy, offering an alternative to the traditions of mathematical logic and formal proof. The new approaches maintain the normative stance of philosophy; they prescribe acceptable forms of thinking based on standards of logic. This contrasts with psychologists' efforts to discover and then to teach students the actual processes used by good thinkers. Philosophers promote an approach designed to *discipline* thinking and to guard against the propensities of humans to accept fallacious arguments and draw inappropriate conclusions. Indeed, the scholarly heart of the informal logic movement is the analysis of fallacies common in undisciplined reasoning.

Most efforts to teach informal logic have focused on college-level courses. Although organized "programs" at this level are uncommon, certain textbooks that are frequently used for informal logic courses provide a reasonable sense of the field (see Johnson, 1981, and Johnson and Blair, 1980, for reviews and analyses of several of these texts). The books typically contain examples of texts for analysis and often present techniques for displaying the relationships among various segments of an argument. In most cases, the texts emphasize identification of particular reasoning fallacies and include technical vocabulary for describing argument structures and their associated fallacies. In addition to philosophers, a small number of people from other disciplines are linked to the informal logic movement. For example, rhetoric has become a major element in many English departments; in these programs, courses in writing and composition often concentrate on principles of argument construction (see Lazere, 1982, for one such approach). Some social scientists (e.g., Browne and Keeley, 1981; Hursh et al., 1983) have developed courses and textbooks in critical thinking that share the concerns of the informal logic movement, although not always the particular analytic vocabulary.

Extensive attention to informal logic at the elementary and secondary school levels is quite recent. It has been spurred by the recent press for critical thinking in the schools and by the inclusion of critical thinking components in some states' competency testing programs (e.g., California, Connecticut, and New Jersey). The only fully developed and extensively assessed program for precollege students is Matthew Lipman's Philosophy for Children. Philosophy for Children's basic teaching method is extensive discussion organized around issues raised in the course of storylike texts. These texts pose traditional philosophical problems—problems of meaning, truth, aesthetics, reality and imagination, ethics, and the like. In this context, a variety of informal logic skills—all focused on logical relations as expressed in ordinary language—are expected to be developed. The oldest and most widely used text, *Harry Stottlemeier's Discovery* (Lipman, 1974/1982), is aimed at fifth- and sixth-grade students. Texts exist for younger and older students as well.

This brief consideration cannot do justice to the variety of practice and range of opinion in the critical thinking and informal logic movement. For example, some programs focus largely on identifying and correctly labeling reasoning fallacies; others concentrate more on developing skills of argumentation in extended discourse, without extensive formal analysis. An important debate in the field exactly parallels psychologists' discussions of whether general cognitive skills or specific knowledge is most central to intellectual competence. Most informal logic philosophers believe that general reasoning capacity can be shaped and that it transcends specific knowledge domains (e.g., Ennis, 1980, 1985). In an even stronger claim, Paul (1982, in press) argues that we should seek to develop in students a broadly rational personality rather than any set of technical reasoning skills. This view usually, but not always, supports calls for independent critical thinking courses. However, a competing view, most strongly stated by McPeck (1981), argues that no general reasoning skill is possible and that all instruction in thinking should be situated in particular disciplines. Despite their parallel concerns, psychologists studying the teachability of cognitive skills and philosophers promoting critical thinking instruction have communicated very little with one another. That is beginning to change, with each group expressing more interest in the other's work (e.g., Norris, 1985; Perkins, 1982), and more mutual influence is probable in the future.

The college-level courses discussed here have enjoyed little or no formal assessment apart from regular course examinations. There is an implicit claim that the kinds of analysis taught in informal logic courses can and should permeate performance throughout the university curriculum, although this has not been tested empirically. As in the case of science, math, and engineering problem-solving courses, then, judgments of the educational importance of university-level informal logic courses must depend for the moment on the extent to which the forms of argument analysis taught are judged to be valuable aspects of learning in their own right. Several evaluations of Philosophy for Children, most of which were conducted by evaluators not directly connected with program development or implementation, provide evidence that the program—when well implemented and given adequate time in the instructional calendar—can produce rather general gains on tests, including improvement on reading comprehension and IQ scores (Lipman, 1985). This program, then, more than most, has been subjected to evaluations on a transfer criterion and has fared quite well.

Problems of Assessment: Some General Comments

Before summarizing the evidence on the teachability of general thinking skills, it is important to reflect on the question of what constitutes appropriate evaluation of programs designed to teach problem-solving and reasoning skills. The most common evaluation reported for the programs we have considered is mastery performance (Arbitman-Smith et al., 1984), that is, performance on exercises *similar to those included in the program itself.* In other words, evaluation provides evidence that students who have used a program learn to do the things the program teaches. This is a necessary first evaluation step, a minimal test that the program in question is worthwhile. Although necessary, such evidence is rarely sufficient to establish the program's educational value. If the program teaches skills that are in themselves considered valuable, then clear evidence that students learn and maintain those skills is adequate. But if a program is meant to teach skills that facilitate other learning but are not valued in themselves, then more is needed than merely tests of the performances directly taught. In these cases, assessments of transfer beyond the course or program itself must be included. Various measures of such transfer can be used, including standardized test scores, subsequent grade point averages, measures of course retention, or advanced program placement. What matters is that the ultimate measures assess socially valued performances.

There are strong theoretical and practical reasons for this. Even when two measures have been correlated repeatedly—for example, Scholastic Aptitude Test (SAT) scores and college grades—nothing guarantees that the correlation will still exist if conditions leading to high scores in either measure are changed. Under normal learning conditions it is safe and practical to treat SAT scores as an indicator of probable college grades. But if special, targeted training produces an increase in SAT scores, one cannot safely assume that college grades will also go up. The correlation was established under particular learning conditions; if those conditions change, the correlation must be reestablished by verifying empirically that the program producing increased SAT scores also produces increased college grades. The same is true for metacognitive skills associated with reading. We know that students who perform well on standardized reading tests usually exhibit more metacognitive behaviors such as elaborating on what the text says, summarizing as they read, and raising questions. But this does not necessarily mean that if we teach students to elaborate, to summarize, and to ask questions, their reading test scores will go up. Useful evaluations of higher order skill training programs require that the educational outcomes of interest be directly assessed. We cannot afford to rely on evidence that certain performances traditionally associated with strong educational outcomes have improved.

On this criterion, even reading tests, probably the most frequently used measure in the studies reviewed, are somewhat problematic. These tests examine abilities that are themselves valued. They are thus better for evaluation purposes than intelligence tests. However, many of the higher order training programs aspire to types and levels of cognitive functioning to which standardized reading tests are not likely to be adequately sensitive. How, for example, should we assess whether skills of argument analysis have permeated students' study of the social sciences or their reading of the daily newspapers? How can we determine whether the problem-solving skills taught in a high school or freshman college course have altered performance in science courses or on-the-job creativity? A crude (and not infrequently used) indicator of academic improvement is course grades. But even grades are only indirect indicators of changed cognitive abilities. They do not reveal the *quality* of thinking, and they offer no indications of transfer beyond purely academic settings.

Clearly, a most important challenge facing the movement for increasing higher order skill learning in the schools is the development of appropriate evaluation strategies. Part of the problem is our penchant for testing. American pressures for standardized testing, especially at the elementary and secondary school levels, make it difficult for curriculum reforms that do not produce test score gains to survive. But most current tests favor students who have acquired lots of factual knowledge and do little to assess either the coherence and utility of that knowledge or the students' ability to use it to reason, solve problems, and the like. To the extent that educators are motivated to produce high test scores, such tests can have the effect of suppressing efforts to expand higher order skill teaching. As interest in thinking and reasoning skills has increased, there has been growing effort to include thinking and reasoning in the batteries of tests given to students. Several states now have or will soon have such tests as part of their state competency testing programs. So far, however, these tests appear to be very limited vehicles for assessing or promoting the kinds of higher order thinking discussed here. They consist mostly of isolated items that test students' critical thinking and reasoning knowledge. But they do not provide the scope or the opportunity for students to carry out extended analyses, to solve open-ended problems, or to display command of complex relationships, although these abilities are at the heart of higher order competence. It seems likely that assessments of forms of thinking that we recognize to involve nuance, judgment, and weighing of alternatives rather than fixed answers will require techniques that themselves depend on judgment and that are open to alternative interpretations.

THINKING IN THE CURRICULUM

How can we summarize the evidence reviewed in the preceding section, and what does it suggest to educators wishing to improve their students' thinking abilities? It is clear that if we were to demand solid empirical evidence supporting a particular approach to higher order skill development before implementing educational programs, we would be condemned at this time to inaction. There is far less empirical evidence of any kind available than we might have imagined and the evidence we have is often of limited utility. In most cases, the evidence amounts mainly to data showing that students who have taken particular courses are more likely to perform well on the tasks directly taught in the courses than students who have not taken those courses. Only a few studies have assessed the key

question of generalization to other parts of the school curriculum or
out-of-school performance.

Although we cannot offer a "seal of approval" for any particular approach, the cumulative evidence justifies cautious optimism
for the venture as a whole. Thinking and problem-solving programs
within the academic disciplines seem to meet their internal goals and
perhaps even boost performance more generally. It seems possible to
raise reading competence by a variety of methods, ranging from study
skill training through the reciprocal teaching methods of Brown and
Palincsar to the discussions of philosophical texts in Lipman's program. On the other hand, general improvements in problem-solving,
rhetoric, or other general thinking abilities have rarely been demonstrated, perhaps because few evaluators have included convincing
assessments of these abilities in their studies.

Most programs reviewed here represent efforts to improve thinking skills through the addition of special courses or course units
rather than through the modification of the mainline curriculum.*
They thus offer a reasonable current estimate of how effective we can
expect separate thinking and reasoning courses to be. As we have
seen, although the available evidence does not establish that such
courses can produce broad transfer of learning, neither does it allow
us to strongly reject the separate course as an element in an educational reform program aimed at improving higher order abilities
in students. Based on present evidence, general course effectiveness
seems to depend on the extent to which it is accompanied by parallel
efforts across the curriculum.

Embedding Thinking Skills in Academic Disciplines

In this view, prudent educational practice should seek to embed efforts to teach cognitive skills into one or another—preferably
all—of the traditional school disciplines, and it should do this regardless of what may also be done in the way of special courses in
thinking or learning skills. This discipline-embedded approach has
several advantages. First, it provides a natural knowledge base and
environment in which to practice and develop higher order skills. As
we have shown earlier, cognitive research has established the very

---

*Some of the discipline-based problem-solving programs and some of the
reading and self-monitoring programs represent important exceptions. The
implications of these programs will be discussed further in subsequent sections.

important role of knowledge in reasoning and thinking. One cannot reason in the abstract; one must reason about something. Each school discipline provides extensive reasoning and problem-solving material by incorporating problem-solving or critical thinking training into the disciplines; the problem of "empty thinking"—thinking about nothing—is solved. As knowledge in the discipline develops, the base on which effective problem solving can operate is naturally available.

Second, embedding higher order skill training within school disciplines provides criteria for what constitutes good thinking and reasoning within the disciplinary tradition. Each discipline has characteristic ways of reasoning, and a complete higher order education would seek to expose students to all of these. Reasoning and problem solving in the physical sciences, for example, are shaped by particular combinations of inductive and deductive reasoning, by appeal to mathematical tests, and by an extensive body of agreed upon fact for which new theories must account. In the social sciences, good reasoning and problem solving are much more heavily influenced by traditions of rhetorical argument, of weighing alternatives, and of "building a case" for a proposed solution. Mathematics insists on formal proofs—a criterion absent in most other disciplines. Each style of reasoning (and several others that could be elaborated) is worth learning. However, only if higher order skills are taught within each discipline are they likely to be learned.

Finally, teaching higher order skills within the disciplines will ensure that something worthwhile will have been learned even if wide transfer proves unattainable. This point is profoundly important. It amounts to saying that no special, separate brief for teaching higher order skills need be made. Rather, it proposes that if a subject matter is worth teaching in school it is worth teaching at a high level—to everyone. A decision to pursue such an approach would transform the whole curriculum in fundamental ways. It would treat higher order skills development as the paramount goal of *all* schooling. Paradoxically, then, dropping the quest for general skills might, in the end, be the most powerful means of cultivating generally higher levels of cognitive functioning.

Saying that thinking skills should be incorporated into existing or planned disciplinary courses is by no means suggesting an easy path. We know less than we need to about how to do this job. Traditional formulations of the issue largely interfere with the kind of inventive educational thought and experimentation that will be needed to turn classes in mathematics, history, physics, or English into arenas for teaching thinking and reasoning abilities. For example, the classic distinction between knowledge as something one reasons *about* and skills as something one reasons *with* has, in practice, placed process skills and knowledge in competition for limited instructional time. The idea that certain forms of knowledge can be powerful tools for learning and problem solving, or that processes and procedures are an expression of principled knowledge, is something that scholars and educators can agree on but have not really found ways to act on. (See Bransford, in press, for a particularly perspicacious analysis of this problem.) Instead, we have had reactive pendulum swings of attention either to process skills ("doing science," "doing history," etc.) or to building large bodies of knowledge. Research and experimentation focusing on how to truly combine these are badly needed.

Higher Order Approaches to the Enabling Disciplines

A particularly powerful way to begin transforming the school program is to concentrate on those parts of the traditional curriculum that enable learning and thinking in many fields. Reading is such an enabling discipline. So is writing, along with, perhaps, skills for effective oral communication. Mathematics is another candidate. Math is involved in many other disciplines, and skills of "mathematization," that is, the construction of formal representations and arguments, could be broadly enabling. The "3-Rs," then, come off rather well on this enabling criterion, although the reading, 'riting, and 'rithmetic curriculum called for in this higher order perspective will look quite different from the traditional hickory stick curriculum. Furthermore, it seems appropriate to add a "fourth R"—reasoning— to our list of potential enabling disciplines. Let us consider each of these briefly.

We have already discussed some current research that points to possibilities for changing the ways in which reading is taught. Thus far the research has shown mainly how very weak readers can be brought up to at least average performance levels. It is important to engage these students in meaning construction activities based on text in settings that incorporate modeling of good performance, lots of feedback, and opportunities to do small bits of the task in the context of seeing the whole job accomplished. However, we do not know for certain that these same methods are all that are needed to raise average performance levels to true high literacy levels. Finding out what is needed to meet this goal is one important agenda for future research. Cognitive researchers about to embark on studies of this important topic would do well to examine the instruction in the high literacy academy tradition for strong hypotheses about the kinds of teaching likely to succeed.

The school curriculum has neglected writing for some time. Its potential role as a cultivator and an enabler of higher order thinking is very great, especially if we consider writing as an occasion to think through arguments and to master forms of reasoning and persuasion that are valued in various disciplines. Existing research clearly shows that children's—and perhaps many teachers'—conceptions of writing do not match what both skilled writers and cognitive research on writing tell us about the process. Children, and unskilled writers generally, tend to view composition as a matter of writing down what they know; Scardamalia and Bereiter (1985) call this the "knowledge telling" strategy of writing. Children are not aware of the role, or even of the existence, of the various discourse conventions and structures good writers use and readers expect (see Stein, 1986, for a review). Finally, they do not think of writing as a problem-solving process (cf. Flower and Hayes, 1980) in which plans must be made for communicating an organized point of view to an audience, and they do not understand that revision is integral to effective writing. Considerable research on the learning and teaching of writing is now underway, some of it focused on writing as a general tool for constructing and expressing arguments. Although the approaches being tried are extremely varied, most reflect a general point of view similar to the one underlying the successful approaches to teaching reading as a higher order skill. They treat writing as an *intentional* process, one in which the writer manages a variety of mental resources—linguistic knowledge, topical knowledge, knowledge of rhetorical forms, processes of attention and judgment—to construct a message that will have a desired impact on a reader. We now need research that focuses explicitly on cultivating and assessing these broad skills of meaning construction and interpretation. As in the case of reading, examination of traditional instruction in rhetoric and related fields should provide a profitable point of departure.

Mathematics must be discussed in somewhat different terms than reading and writing. It is not only an enabling skill, widely called on in a number of other disciplines, but also a discipline in its own right whose particular knowledge structures must be learned. Mathematics also poses special problems, derived from its heavy dependence on formal notations. This has the effect of making it difficult for students to use their informal and intuitive knowledge of mathematical concepts to support school mathematics learning and to advance their mathematical competence. As we noted earlier, good evidence suggests that much school mathematics learning proceeds as a matter of memorizing rules for formal symbol manipulation without much understanding of why the rules work as they do or what the symbols stand for. If education were concerned only with the calculation skills needed to "get by" in routine jobs and family obligations, this would not cause much concern. But a high literacy approach to mathematics teaching cannot afford to let this separation between symbols and meaning, between calculation and mathematical reasoning, survive. Although many mathematics educators have sought ways of making particular concepts and procedures more understandable to children, to date no research has directly addressed the question of how a broad meaning-construction approach to mathematics learning can be promoted among all students—so that students themselves come to seek the connections between formal notations and their justifying concepts. This remains a major agenda for research leading to a higher order approach to mathematics teaching.

Reasoning has never had an explicit place in the mass education curriculum. Philosophy has no regular position in the standard American high school curriculum, nor is reasoning specified as part of the elementary school syllabus in the way reading, writing, and mathematics are. By contrast, both have been cornerstones of the elite, academy education tradition. Thus, incorporating reasoning into the regular educational program would extend the high literacy tradition to the entire school system. However, it is not clear whether reasoning should be treated as a separate discipline or suffused through the curriculum. Most philosophers working within the informal logic movement want to see critical thinking or reasoning courses included in the curriculum. Their argument is partly practical: reasoning skills will be passed over or trivialized if they are spread through the curriculum and not given formal recognition. But there is also a theoretical argument for treating reasoning as a separate enabling discipline; this is that principles of logical reasoning are unitary, not specific to particular domains of knowledge (see Paul, in press, responding to a contrary argument by McPeck, 1981). Currently, we have no empirical evidence to support the idea that teaching people to recognize and analyze reasoning fallacies—a core element in most critical thinking and informal logic curricula—in fact leads them to avoid such fallacies in their own thinking. Without careful attention to this problem, informal logic could become just another body of knowledge—perhaps judged valuable in its own right but without claim to a special role in the general development of higher order thinking and learning capabilities. We need, then, substantial new research, requiring the collaboration of philosophers and cognitive scientists, to identify approaches to teaching reasoning that actually improve reasoning performance either in academic disciplines or in practical situations.

CULTIVATING THE DISPOSITION TO HIGHER ORDER THINKING

It has been convenient to examine teaching programs in several distinct categories. Yet there are striking points of similarity among those programs that have shown some promising results. Many such programs rely on a social setting and social interaction for much of teaching and practice. Although one can imagine individually worked exercises designed to improve aspects of thinking skill, very few programs in fact propose such activities. Instead, students are encouraged to work problems in pairs or in small groups. Instructors may also orchestrate special discussion and practice sessions. When investigators of different theoretical orientations and disciplinary backgrounds converge on a common prescription in this way, we should consider what shared intuition may be at work. What roles might social interaction be playing in the development of thinking? The authors cited in the preceding pages mention several possibilities.

First, the social setting provides occasions for *modeling* effective thinking strategies. Skilled thinkers (often the instructor but sometimes more advanced fellow students) can demonstrate desirable ways of attacking problems, analyzing texts, and constructing arguments. This process opens normally hidden mental activities to inspection. Through observing others, students can become aware of mental processes that might otherwise have remained entirely implicit. Research suggests, however, that modeling alone does not produce very powerful results. If students only watched more skilled thinkers perform, they would not substantially improve their own thinking.

Apparently there is more to learning in a social setting than watching others perform. "Thinking aloud" in a social setting allows others—peers or an instructor—to critique and shape one's performance, something that cannot be done effectively if only the results but not the processes of thought are visible. The social setting may also provide a kind of scaffolding for an individual learner's initially limited performance. Instead of practicing small bits of thinking in isolation with no sense of each bit's significance to the task as a whole, a group solves a problem, or writes a composition, or analyzes an argument together. Within the group, extreme novices can participate in performing complex tasks. If things go well, they can eventually take over most or all of the work themselves, with a developed appreciation of how individual elements in the process contribute to the whole. This theory, adapted from Vygotsky (1978), is embodied explicitly in the reciprocal teaching of Palincsar and Brown, and variants of it have been proposed by a number of other investigators (e.g., Collins et al., in press).

The social setting may also function to motivate students. Students are encouraged to try new, more active approaches, and they receive social support even for partially successful efforts. Through this process, students come to think of themselves as capable of engaging in independent thinking and of exercising control over their learning processes. The public setting also lends social status and validation to what can perhaps best be called the *disposition* to higher order thinking. The term disposition should not be taken to imply a biological or inherited trait. As used here, it is more akin to a *habit* of thought, one that can be learned and, therefore, taught. Engaging in higher order thinking with others seems likely to teach students that they have the ability, the permission, and even the obligation to engage in a kind of critical analysis that does not always accept problem formulations as presented or that may challenge an accepted position.

We have good reason to believe that shaping this disposition to critical thought is central to developing higher order cognitive abilities in students. Research on strategy training shows that, if instruction is to work at all, it often works very quickly—in just a few lessons or sometimes with little more than directions to use some strategy. However, people induced to use a particular learning strategy will often do so on the immediate occasion but will fail to apply the same strategy on subsequent occasions. Both of these recurrent findings serve to remind us that much of learning to be a good thinker is learning to recognize and even search for opportunities to apply one's mental capacities (cf. Belmont et al., 1982).

This suggests that the task for those who would raise the intellectual performance levels in children is not just to teach children new cognitive processes but to get them to use those processes widely and frequently. The kind of higher order thinking we have discussed requires elaborating, adding complexity, and going beyond the given to construct new formulations of issues. It also involves weighing multiple alternatives and sometimes accepting uncertainty. As such, higher order thinking requires effort on the part of the individual and may involve some social risk—of disagreeing with others perceived to be more powerful, of not arriving at the expected answers, of not always responding instantly. To overcome these difficulties, educational institutions must cultivate not only skills for thinking but also the disposition to use them.

A widely shared set of implicit assumptions exists about how dispositions for higher order thinking might develop. They center on the role of a social community in establishing norms of behavior, providing opportunity for practice, and providing occasions for learning particular skills. The fundamental theme is that such dispositions are cultivated by participation in social communities that value thinking and independent judgment. Such communities communicate these values by making available many occasions for such activity and responding encouragingly to expressions of questioning and judgment. The process of learning is further aided when there are many opportunities to observe others engaging in such thinking activities. Finally, dispositions for higher order thinking require sustained long-term cultivation; they do not emerge from short-term, quick-fix interventions.

This set of beliefs, although highly plausible, has received little empirical investigation. On the whole, research on the development of cognitive abilities has proceeded quite separately from research on social and personality development. For example, the extensive body of childhood socialization research (Hetherington, 1983) says much about the emergence of traits such as aggressiveness, dependency, conformity, or gender identification, but it says little about how intellectual tendencies develop. An interesting new research project (Caplan, 1985) on the development of intellectual curiosity in young children appears to be a first link between research on child socialization and our present concern for shaping higher order thinking dispositions.

"Cognitive styles" (e.g., Messick, 1976) such as reflectivity are known to be related to school performance, and efforts have been made to shape reflectivity (e.g., Meichenbaum, 1985). But this research has not generally attended to the qualitative aspects of intellectual performance, and it is impossible to know whether higher order thinking was in fact improved. Other research on improving persistence (e.g., Turkewitz et al., 1975) has tended to measure how much work students do but not whether they engage in complex cognitive activities. Some recent research on intrinsic motivation may help tie motivation to the quality as well as the quantity of educational work (see Lepper, 1981, 1983; Nicholls, 1983). When people work to gain praise, grades, or material benefits, they are externally motivated. When they work to master a task, they are intrinsically motivated. Apparently some correlation exists between the kinds of motivations that keep people working and several qualitative features of their work: for example, the complexity of the tasks they choose to work on, the range of material to which they attend, and the extent to which they are able to shift direction ("break set") to pursue a new, more fruitful approach (Condry and Chambers, 1981; Kruglanski, 1981; Lepper and Greene, 1981; McGraw, 1981).

A promising link between quality of thinking and persistence is being forged by investigators studying differences in people's conceptions of ability. For example, Dweck and her colleagues (Dweck, in press; Dweck and Elliot, 1983) have shown that individuals differ fundamentally in their conceptions of intelligence and that these conceptions mediate very different ways of attacking problems. A distinction is made between two competing conceptions of ability, or "theories of intelligence," that people may hold. One, called the *entity* conception, treats ability as a global, stable quality. The second, called the *incremental* conception, treats ability as a repertoire of skills that can be expanded through efforts to learn. Entity conceptions orient children toward *performing* well so that they can display their intelligence and toward not revealing lack of ability by giving "wrong" responses. Incremental conceptions orient children toward *learning* well so that they can acquire new knowledge or skill. Most relevant to the present argument, incremental conceptions of ability and associated learning goals lead children to analyze tasks and to formulate strategies for overcoming difficulties. We can easily recognize these as close cousins to the kinds of higher order thinking discussed in this essay. In a related analysis, Covington (1983) suggests that people who view ability as created through strategic self-management (of study time, of types of elaboration, of ways of attacking tasks) will be better able to compensate for self-attributions of low initial ability.

A key question, of course, is whether these differences in type of motivation or theory of intelligence can be deliberately shaped by the way in which school activity is organized. Evidence suggests that the nature of the environment in which one works makes a difference in whether one invokes internal or external motivations for one's work. However, research has not examined whether personal traits favoring internal motivation can be developed by deliberately altering institutional or social patterns. Very recent work by Dweck and her colleagues is examining ways of helping students to acquire and apply incremental conceptions of intelligence, but more extensive research is required before clear conclusions can be drawn. In any case, these lines of motivation research highlight the possibilities for an important convergence between efforts aimed at teaching higher order cognitive skills and those aimed at cultivating dispositions to apply those skills.

SUMMARY AND CONCLUSIONS

What Are Higher Order Skills?

*Higher order thinking is difficult to define but
easy to recognize when it occurs.*

Higher order thinking involves a cluster of elaborative mental activities requiring nuanced judgment and analysis of complex situations according to multiple criteria. Higher order thinking is effortful and depends on self-regulation. The path of action or correct answers are not fully specified in advance. The thinker's task is to construct meaning and impose structure on situations rather than to expect to find them already apparent.

*Higher order thinking has always been a
major goal of elite educational institutions.
The current challenge is to find ways to teach
higher order thinking within institutions
committed to educating the entire population.*

In its origins, the mass educational system was concerned with routine competencies such as simple computation, reading familiar and predictable texts, and acquiring well-defined vocational competencies. It was not considered necessary or possible for all students to learn to interpret complex texts, write extended arguments, or develop original solutions to problems. However, changing economic and social conditions are now creating a demand for these abilities in all citizens, and schools are seeking ways to cultivate thinking skills in all students. No educational system has ever been built on the assumption that everyone, not just an elite, can become a competent thinker. We must view this new challenge as an invitation to inventive and very demanding educational reform.

> *Higher order thinking is the hallmark of*
> *successful learning at all levels—not only the*
> *more advanced.*

The challenge to reform comes at a time when cognitive research provides an important reconceptualization of the nature of thinking and learning that can inform and guide educational work. The most important single message of this body of research is that complex thinking processes—elaborating the given material, making inferences beyond what is explicitly presented, building adequate representations, analyzing and constructing relationships—are involved in even the most apparently elementary mental activities. Children cannot understand what they read without making inferences and using information that goes beyond what is written in the text. They cannot become good writers without engaging in complex problem-solving-like processes. Basic mathematics will not be effectively learned if children only try to memorize rules for manipulating written numerical symbols. All of this implies that "basic" and "higher order" skills cannot be clearly separated.

> *Good thinking depends on specific knowledge,*
> *but many aspects of powerful thinking*
> *are shared across disciplines and situations.*

A central issue, both for educational practice and for research that can guide that practice, is whether thinking and learning abilities are general—that is, applicable in all domains of thinking—or specific to a particular domain. The evidence shows clearly that thinking is driven by and supported by knowledge, in the form of both specific facts and organizing principles. This knowledge, together with the automated recognition and performance that come with extended practice, allows experts in any field to engage in more sophisticated thinking than people new to the field. At the same time, many aspects of thinking are shared across fields of expertise. These include a wide range of oral and written communication skills, mathematization and representational abilities, principles of reasoning, and skills of argument construction and evaluation. These can be thought of as "enabling skills" for learning and thinking. Generally speaking, people rely on powerful but only narrowly applicable thinking methods in domains in which they are expert and use broadly applicable but weak methods for learning and thinking in fields they know little about. Good thinkers need both the powerful but specific and the general but weak kinds of skills.

Can Higher Order Thinking Be Directly Taught?

Elements of thinking are clearly teachable.

The programs reviewed here show that many components of thinking can be effectively taught. That is, there is evidence that the particular performances taught in the programs are in fact learned by students. The kinds of components that have been successfully taught include generating multiple ideas and alternative viewpoints on a particular topic, generating summaries, skimming, figuring out word meanings from context, solving analogies and logical puzzles, and detecting logical reasoning fallacies.

However, an integrated ability to learn, think,
and reason and a broad disposition to engage
in higher order thinking are not necessarily
ensured by acquiring particular components
of thinking.

We need direct assessments of the kinds of complex reasoning and problem-solving skills that constitute higher order thinking. Most evaluations have not made such assessments. They have relied instead on assessments of particular elements that are taught or on "indicator" tests—such as IQ or SAT scores—that are normally correlated with successful learning and thinking. However, under changed instruction and learning conditions, these traditional indicators may no longer be valid. Thus, we have less evidence than would be desirable, and less than the proliferation of programs would suggest, on whether and how thinking abilities that are integrated and usable can actually be cultivated.

Only a few programs provide convincing
evidence that broadly applicable and
integrated abilities have been acquired.

In the most convincing cases, improvements due to instruction have been demonstrated for reading comprehension, general grade averages, and essay writing. Some programs also demonstrate improved problem-solving or laboratory performance in specific disciplines, especially in mathematics and science, thus meeting their own goals—although not demonstrating (and not necessarily seeking) transfer to other disciplines or to practical life. A larger number of programs point to student claims that they now use the kinds of abilities taught. However, these claims are difficult to evaluate; they show that students generally feel better about their thinking and learning abilities after the course, but they do not tell us whether these improved self-assessments are in fact warranted.

Current testing practices in American
education do not provide very powerful tools
for assessing the effects of efforts to teach
thinking and reasoning. Testing practices may in
fact interfere with cultivation of the kind of
higher order skills that are desired.

In general, the tests used in assessing educational efforts involve multiple choice or other short, precoded answers. These tests can measure the accumulation of knowledge and can be used to examine specific components of reasoning or thinking. However, they are ill suited to assessing the kinds of integrated thinking that we call "higher order." If progress is to be made in converting American schools to the higher order thinking agenda, we must develop forms of assessment that are more suited to the nature of the abilities we seek to teach.

How Should Instruction in Higher Order Thinking Be Organized?

*A broad disposition to higher order thinking
must be cultivated.*

Isolated instruction in thinking skills, no matter how elegant the training provided, is unlikely to produce broadly used thinking ability. Thinking well requires more than knowing a selected set of strategies or techniques for problem solving and learning. It also requires knowing when these strategies are appropriate, and it requires the motivation to apply them, even though they may involve more effort than routine performances as well as some risk of social controversy. This implies that higher order skills must suffuse the school program from kindergarten on and in every subject matter. Training in general skills must be supplemented and supported by application throughout the curriculum. Various subject matters in the school program should be taught with an eye to developing the powerful thinking methods used by experts in those disciplines. Students must come to think of themselves as able and obligated to engage in critical analysis and problem solving throughout schooling. The following are promising directions that educational experimentation might take.

*Embedding instruction in thinking skills
within the academic disciplines of the school
curriculum has several advantages.*

It ensures that there is something solid to reason about. It supplies criteria from within the disciplinary traditions for what constitutes good reasoning and thinking. It ensures that something worthwhile will have been taught and learned even if wide transfer proves impossible. However, there is a caveat for those who seek to embed higher order skills teaching in the existing school program. Thinking skills tend to be driven out of the curriculum by ever-growing demands for teaching larger and larger bodies of knowledge. The idea that knowledge must be acquired first and that its application to reasoning and problem solving can be delayed is a persistent one in educational thinking. "Hierarchies" of educational objectives, although intended to promote attention to higher order skills, paradoxically feed this belief by suggesting that knowledge acquisition is a first stage in a sequence of educational goals. The relative ease of assessing people's knowledge, as opposed to their thought processes, further feeds this tendency in educational practice.

Periodically, educators resist this pressure by proposing that various forms of process- or skill-oriented teaching replace knowledge-oriented instruction. In the past, this has often led to a severe deemphasis of basic subject matter knowledge. This, in turn, has had the effect of alienating many subject matter specialists, creating pendulum swings of educational opinion in which knowledge-oriented and process-oriented programs periodically displace each other, and delaying any serious resolution of the knowledge–process paradox. We cannot allow these pendulum swings to continue. Cognitive research shows the intimate relationship of subject matter knowledge and reasoning processes. We need both practical experimentation in schools and more controlled instructional experimentation in laboratories to discover ways of incorporating our new understanding of the knowledge–reasoning connection into instruction.

> *Reorienting instruction in the 3-Rs
> (the "enabling disciplines") so that they incorporate
> more of the higher order processes seems a
> particularly promising approach to improving
> thinking skills.*

The 3-Rs of the traditional basic school curriculum can become the environment for higher order education. Effective reading, writing, and mathematics learning depend on elaboration, explication, and various forms of meaning construction. Reorienting basic instruction in these curricula to focus on intentional, self-managed learning and strategies for meaning construction, rather than on routinized performances, will result in more effective basic skill instruction while providing a strong base for higher order skill development in other disciplines.

> *A fourth "R"—reasoning—might be considered
> a candidate for a new enabling discipline
> in the school curriculum.*

Many philosophers argue that principles of logical reasoning are unitary and not specific to particular domains of knowledge. The study of reasoning, they claim, can enable effective thinking across disciplines. Although there has been little empirical investigation of this claim, the hypothesis is a reasonable one and should be investigated carefully. A potential pitfall is that learning to identify reasoning fallacies—a core element of most programs in informal logic and critical thinking—may not in fact help people improve their own reasoning. This question needs careful attention, with appropriate evaluation of the extent to which students in reasoning courses learn to produce, as well as analyze, reasoned arguments.

Links between thinking skills and motivation
for thinking must be developed.

Everyone agrees that successful educational achievement requires both motivation and appropriate cognitive activity. Yet our theories implicitly treat motivation and cognition as if they worked independently to determine the nature and extent of learning. In fact, these traditionally separate factors appear far more intimately related than most current research helps us to appreciate.* However, recent research linking children's conceptions of their own and others' intelligence to the ways in which they analyze learning tasks offers a promising new connection, as does research on intrinsic motivation for learning. Active experimentation on what kinds of school activity organization cultivate motivation for particular kinds of complex and strategic learning is needed. The two concerns must be merged as this work proceeds; efforts to develop more intellectually functional motivational patterns should not become substitutes for efforts to establish specific cognitive competencies. Motivation for learning will be empty if substantive cognitive abilities are not developed, and the cognitive abilities will remain unused if the disposition to thinking is not developed.

---

*The monograph by Cole and Griffen (1987) explores this question extensively from another angle, focusing on the social context for thinking. The present monograph and Cole and Griffen's study provide complementary vantage points for addressing this key set of issues.

References

Arbitman-Smith, R., Haywood, H. C., and Bransford, J. D. (1984). Assessing cognitive change. In P. Brooks, R. Sperber, and C. N. McCauley (Eds.), *Learning and cognition in the mentally retarded* (pp. 433–472). Hillsdale, NJ: Erlbaum.

Belmont, J. M., Butterfield, E. C., and Ferretti, R. P. (1982). To secure transfer of training, instruct self-management skills. In D. K. Detterman and R. J. Sternberg (Eds.), *How and how much can intelligence be increased?* (pp. 147–154). Norwood, NJ: Ablex.

Bereiter, C., and Bird, M. (1985). Use of thinking aloud in identification and teaching of reading comprehension strategies. *Cognition and Instruction, 2,* 131–156.

Bereiter, C., and Scardamalia, M. (1982). From conversation to composition: The role of instruction in a developmental process. In R. Glaser (Ed.), *Advances in instructional psychology* (Vol. 2, pp. 1–64). Hillsdale, NJ: Erlbaum.

Bolt Beranek and Newman. (1983). *Final report, Project Intelligence: The development of procedures to enhance thinking skills.* Cambridge, MA: Bolt Beranek and Newman Laboratories, Inc.

Bransford, J. D. (In press). *Enhancing thinking and learning.* San Francisco: Freeman and Co.

Brown, A. L., Bransford, J. D., Ferrara, R. A., and Campione, J. C. (1983). Learning, remembering, and understanding. In J. H. Flavell and E. M. Markman (Eds.), *Cognitive development* (Vol. III of P. H. Mussen, Ed., *Handbook of child psychology,* pp. 77–166). New York: Wiley.

Brown, J. S., and Van Lehn, K. (1980). Repair theory: A generative theory of "bugs." In T. P. Carpenter, J. M. Moser, and T. A. Romberg (Eds.), *Addition and subtraction: A cognitive perspective* (pp. 117–135). Hillsdale, NJ: Erlbaum.

Browne, M. N., and Keeley, S. N. (1981). *Asking the right questions.* Englewood Cliffs, NJ: Prentice-Hall.

Bureau of Education. (1918). *Cardinal principles of secondary education* (Bull. No. 35). Washington, DC: Department of the Interior.

Caplan, J. S. (1985, April). *The development of intellectual curiosity.* Paper presented at the meeting of the Society for Research in Child Development, Toronto, Canada.

Carraher, T. N., Carraher, D. W., and Schliemann, A. D. (1985). Mathematics in the streets and in schools. *British Journal of Developmental Psychology, 3,* 21–29.

Clement, J. (1982). Algebra word problem solutions: Thought processes underlying a common misconception. *Journal of Research in Mathematics Education, 13,* 16–30.

Cole, M., and Griffen, P. (Eds.). (1987). *Contextual factors in education: Improving science and math education for minorities and women.* Madison, WI: Wisconsin Center for Educational Research.

College Entrance Examination Board. (1983). *Academic preparation for college.* New York: College Entrance Examination Board.

Collins, A., Gentner, D., and Rubin, A. (1981). *Teaching study strategies* (Rep. No. 4794). Cambridge, MA: Bolt Beraneck and Newman Laboratories, Inc.

Collins, A., and Smith, E. E. (1982). Teaching the process of reading comprehension. In D. Detterman and R. Sternberg (Eds.), *How much and how can intelligence be increased?* (pp. 173–185). Norwood, NJ: Ablex.

Collins, A., Brown, J. S., and Newman, S. E. (In press). Teaching the craft of reading, writing, and mathematics. In L. B. Resnick (Ed.), *Knowing and learning: Issues for a cognitive science of instruction.* Hillsdale, NJ: Erlbaum.

Condry, J., and Chambers, J. (1981). Intrinsic motivation and the process of learning. In M. R. Lepper and D. Greene (Eds.), *The hidden costs of reward* (pp. 61–84). Hillsdale, NJ: Erlbaum.

Covington, M. V. (1983). Motivated cognitions. In S. G. Paris, G. M. Olson, and H. W. Stevenson (Eds.), *Learning and motivation in the classroom* (pp. 139–164). Hillsdale, NJ: Erlbaum.

Covington, M. V. (1985). Strategic thinking and the fear of failure. In J. W. Segal, S. F. Chipman, and R. Glaser (Eds.), *Thinking and learning skills: Vol. 1. Relating instruction to research* (pp. 389–416). Hillsdale, NJ: Erlbaum.

Covington, M. V. (In press). Instruction in problem-solving planning. In S. L. Friedman, E. K. Scholnick, and R. R. Cocking (Eds.), *Blueprints for thinking: The role of planning in cognitive development.* Cambridge, England: Cambridge University Press.

Dansereau, D. F. (1985). Learning strategy research. In J. W. Segal, S. F. Chipman, and R. Glaser (Eds.), *Thinking and learning skills: Vol. 1. Relating instruction to research* (pp. 209–239). Hillsdale, NJ: Erlbaum.

Day, J. D. (1980). *Training summarization skills: A comparison of teaching methods.* Unpublished doctoral dissertation, University of Illinois.

de Bono, E. (1970). *Lateral thinking.* New York: Harper & Row.

de Bono, E. (1976). *Teaching thinking.* London: Temple Smith.

de Bono, E. (1985). The CoRT thinking program. In J. W. Segal, S. F. Chipman, and R. Glaser (Eds.), *Thinking and learning skills: Vol. 1. Relating instruction to research* (pp. 363–388). Hillsdale, NJ: Erlbaum.

Dehn, N., and Schank, R. (1982). Artificial and human intelligence. In R. J. Sternberg (Ed.), *Handbook of human intelligence* (pp. 353–391). Cambridge, MA: Harvard University Press.

de Kleer, J., and Brown, J. S. (1980). Mental models of physical mechanisms and their acquisition. In J. R. Anderson (Ed.), *Cognitive skills and their acquisition* (pp. 285–309). Hillsdale, NJ: Erlbaum.

Dweck, C. S. (In press). Motivation. In R. Glaser and A. Lesgold (Eds.), *The handbook of psychology and education* (Vol. 1). Hillsdale, NJ: Erlbaum.

Dweck, C. S., and Elliot, E. S. (1983). Achievement motivation. In E. M. Hetherington (Ed.), *Socialization, personality, and social development* (Vol. IV of P. H. Mussen, Ed., *Handbook of child psychology*, pp. 643–692). New York: Wiley.

Edwards, J., Baldauf, R. B., and Cook, J. (1984, August). *The effects of a thinking skills program on students.* Paper presented at the Conference on Thinking, Harvard University, Cambridge, Massachusetts.

Ennis, R. H. (1980). A conception of rational thinking. In J. Coombs (Ed.), *Philosophy of education 1979* (pp. 3–30). Normal, IL: Philosophy of Education Society.

Ennis, R. H. (1985). Critical thinking and the curriculum. *National Forum, 65*(1), 28–31.

Feuerstein, R., Jensen, M. R., Hoffman, M. B., and Rand, Y. (1985). Instrumental enrichment, an intervention program for structural cognitive modifiability: Theory and practice. In J. W. Segal, S. F. Chipman, and R. Glaser (Eds.), *Thinking and learning skills: Vol. 1. Relating instruction to research* (pp. 43–82). Hillsdale, NJ: Erlbaum.

Flower, L. S., and Hayes, J. R. (1980). The dynamics of composing: Making plans and juggling constraints. In L. Gregg and E. Steinberg (Eds.), *Cognitive processes in writing: An interdisciplinary approach* (pp. 31–50). Hillsdale, NJ: Erlbaum.

Fuller, M. (1975, June). *Teaching the process of problem solving.* Paper presented at Annual Conference, American Society for Engineering Education, Colorado State University, Fort Collins, Colorado.

Fuller, M. (1978). *Reasoning for experimenters.* Paper presented at Frontiers in Education Conference, Orlando, Florida.

Gelman, R., and Gallistel, C. R. (1978). *The child's understanding of number.* Cambridge, MA: Harvard University Press.

Ginsburg, H. A. (1977). *Children's arithmetic: The learning process.* New York: Van Nostrand Reinhold.

Glaser, R. (1984). Education and thinking: The role of knowledge. *American Psychologist, 39,* 93–104.

Groen, G., and Parkman, J. M. (1972). A chronometric analysis of simple addition. *Psychological Review, 79,* 329–343.

Hayes, J. R. (1981). *The complete problem solver.* Philadelphia: Franklin Institute Press.

Hetherington, E. M. (1983). *Socialization, personality, and social development.* (Vol. IV of P. H. Mussen, Ed., *Handbook of child psychology*). New York: Wiley.

Hiebert, J., and Wearne, D. (1985). A model of students' decimal computation procedures. *Cognition and Instruction 2,* 175–205.

Hursh, B., Haas, P., and Moore, M. (1983). An interdisciplinary model to implement general education. *Journal of Higher Education,* 54(1), 42–59.

Johnson, R. H. (1981). The new logic course: The state of the art in non-formal methods of argument analysis. *Teaching Philosophy,* 4(2), 123–143.

Johnson, R. H., and Blair, J. A. (1980). The recent development of informal logic. In J. A. Blair and R. H. Johnson (Eds.), *Informal logic* (pp. 3–28). Pt. Reyes, CA: Edgepress.

Jones, B. F., Amiran, M., and Katims, M. (1985). Teaching cognitive strategies and text structures within language arts programs. In J. W. Segal, S. F. Chipman, and R. Glaser (Eds.), *Thinking and learning skills: Vol. 1. Relating instruction to research* (pp. 259–296). Hillsdale, NJ: Erlbaum.

Jones, B. F., Friedman, L. B., Tinzmann, M., and Cox, B. E. (1984). *Content-driven comprehension instruction and assessment: A model for Army-training literature.* (Tech. Rep.). Alexandria, VA: Army Research Institute.

Journal of Educational Psychology. (1921). Intelligence and its measurement: A symposium. *The Journal,* 12, 123–147, 195–216.

Just, M. A., and Carpenter, P. A. (1980). A theory of reading: From eye fixations to comprehension. *Psychological Review,* 87, 329–354.

Kintsch, W. (1979). On modeling comprehension. *Educational Psychologist,* 14, 3–14.

Kruglanski, A. W. (1981). Endogenous attribution and intrinsic motivation. In M. R. Lepper and D. Greene (Eds.), *The hidden costs of reward* (pp. 85–108). Hillsdale, NJ: Erlbaum.

Larkin, J. H., McDermott, J., Simon, D. P., and Simon, H. (1980). Expert and novice performance in solving physics problems. *Science,* 208, 1335–1342.

Lazere, D. (1982). *Composition for critical thinking: A course description.* San Louis Obispo, CA: California Polytechnical State University Press.

Lepper, M. R. (1981). Intrinsic and extrinsic motivation in children: Detrimental effects of superfluous social controls. In W. A. Collins (Ed.), *Minnesota symposium on child psychology* (Vol. 14, pp. 155–214). Hillsdale, NJ: Erlbaum.

Lepper, M. R. (1983). Extrinsic reward and intrinsic motivation: Implications for the classroom. In J. M. Levine and M. C. Wang (Eds.), *Teacher and student perceptions: Implications for learning* (pp. 281–318). Hillsdale, NJ: Erlbaum.

Lepper, M. R., and Greene, D. (1981). Overjustification research and beyond: Toward a means–end analysis of intrinsic and extrinsic motivation. In M. R. Lepper and D. Greene (Eds.), *The hidden costs of reward* (pp. 109–148). Hillsdale, NJ: Erlbaum.

Lipman, M. (1982). *Harry Stottlemeier's discovery.* Philadelphia: Temple University Press. (Original work published in 1974.)

Lipman, M. (1985). Thinking skills fostered by philosophy for children. In J. W. Segal, S. F. Chipman, and R. Glaser (Eds.), *Thinking and learning skills: Vol. 1. Relating instruction to research* (pp. 83–108). Hillsdale, NJ: Erlbaum.

Lochhead, J. (1985). Teaching analytical reasoning skills through pair problem solving. In J. W. Segal, S. F. Chipman, and R. Glaser (Eds.), *Thinking and learning skills: Vol. 1. Relating instruction to research* (pp. 109–132). Hillsdale, NJ: Erlbaum.

Mandl, H., Stein, N. L., and Trabasso, T. (Eds.). (1984). *Learning and comprehension of text.* Hillsdale, NJ: Erlbaum.

Matz, M. (1982). Towards a process model for high school algebra errors. In D. Sleeman and J. S. Brown (Eds.), *Intelligent tutoring systems* (pp. 25–50). New York: Academic Press.

McGraw, K. O. (1981). The detrimental effects of reward on performance: A literature review and a prediction model. In M. R. Lepper and D. Greene (Eds.), *The hidden costs of reward* (pp. 33–60). Hillsdale, NJ: Erlbaum.

McPeck, J. (1981). *Critical thinking and education.* Oxford, England: Martin Robinson.

Meichenbaum, D. (1985). Teaching thinking: A cognitive-behavioral perspective. In S. F. Chipman, J. W. Segal, and R. Glaser (Eds.), *Thinking and learning skills: Vol. 2. Research and open questions* (pp. 407–426). Hillsdale, NJ: Erlbaum.

Messick, S. (Ed.). (1976). *Individuality in learning.* San Francisco: Jossey-Bass.

National Assessment of Educational Progress (NAEP). (1983). *The third national mathematics assessment: Results, trends and issues* (13-MA-01). Denver, CO: Educational Commission of the States.

Neves, D. M., and Anderson, J. R. (1981). Knowledge compilation: Mechanisms for the automatization of cognitive skills. In J. R. Anderson (Ed.), *Cognitive skills and their acquisition.* Hillsdale, NJ: Erlbaum.

Newell, A., and Estes, W. K. (1983). Cognitive science and artificial intelligence. In Committee on Science, Engineering, and Public Policy (Ed.), *Research briefings 1983.* Washington, DC: National Academy Press.

Newell, A., and Rosenbloom, P. S. (1981). Mechanisms of skill acquisition and the law of practice. In J. R. Anderson (Ed.), *Cognitive skills and their acquisition* (pp. 1–56). Hillsdale, NJ: Erlbaum.

Nicholls, J. G. (1983). Conceptions of ability and achievement motivation: A theory and its implications for education. In S. G. Paris, G. M. Olson, and H. W. Stevenson (Eds.), *Learning and motivation in the classroom* (pp. 211–238). Hillsdale, NJ: Erlbaum.

Nickerson, R. S., Perkins, D., and Smith, E. E. (1985). *The teaching of thinking.* Hillsdale, NJ: Erlbaum.

Norris, S. P. (1985). Thinking about critical thinking: Philosophers can't go it alone. In D. A. Nyberg (Ed.), *Philosophy of education.*

Palincsar, A. S., and Brown, A. L. (1984). Reciprocal teaching of comprehension-fostering and comprehension-monitoring activities. *Cognition and Instruction, 1,* 117–175.

Papert, S. (1980). *Mindstorms.* New York: Basic Books.

Paris, S. G., and Jacobs, J. E. (1984). The benefits of informed instruction for children's reading awareness and comprehension skills. *Child Development, 55,* 2083–2093.

Paris, S. G., Cross, D. R., and Lipson, M. Y. (1984). Informed strategies for learning: A program to improve children's reading awareness and comprehension. *Journal of Educational Psychology, 76,* 1239–1252

Paul, R. (1982). Teaching critical thinking in the "strong" sense: A focus on self-deception, world views, and a dialectical mode of analysis. *Informal Logic, 4,* 3–7.

Paul, R. (In press). A review of *Critical thinking and education. Informal Logic.*

Perfetti, C. (1985). *Reading ability.* New York: Oxford University Press.

Perkins, D. N. (1982). *Difficulties in everyday reasoning and their change with education.* Final Report to the Spencer Foundation, Project Zero, Harvard University.

Peterson, P., Swing, S., Stark, K., and Waas, G. (1984). Student's cognitions and time on task during mathematics instruction. *American Educational Research Journal, 21,* 487–515.

Polson, P. G., and Jeffries, R. (1985). Analysis—instruction in general problem-solving skills: An analysis of four approaches. In J. W. Segal, S. F. Chipman, and R. Glaser (Eds.), *Thinking and learning skills: Vol. 1. Relating instruction to research* (pp. 417–455). Hillsdale, NJ: Erlbaum.

Reif, F., and St. John, M. (1979). Teaching physicists' thinking skills in the laboratory. *American Journal of Physics, 47,* 950–957.

Resnick, D. P. (1980). Minimum competency testing historically considered. *Review of Research in Education, 8,* 3–29.

Resnick, D. P., and Resnick, L. B. (1977). The nature of literacy: An historical exploration. *Harvard Educational Review, 47,* 370–385.

Resnick, L. B. (1987). The development of mathematical intuition. In M. Perlmutter (Ed.), *Minnesota symposium on child psychology* (Vol. 19, pp. 159–194). Hillsdale, NJ: Erlbaum.

Resnick, L. B., Cauzinille-Marmeche, E., and Mathieu, J. (1987). Understanding algebra. In J. Sloboda and D. Rogers (Eds.), *Cognitive processes in mathematics* (pp. 169–203). New York: Oxford University Press.

Rubinstein, M. F. (1980). A decade of experience in teaching an interdisciplinary problem-solving course. In D. T. Tuma and F. Reif (Eds.), *Problem solving and education: Issues in teaching and research* (pp. 25–38). Hillsdale, NJ: Erlbaum.

Scardamalia, M., and Bereiter, C. (1985). Fostering the development of self-regulation in children's knowledge processing. In S. F. Chipman, J. W. Segal, and R. Glaser (Eds.), *Thinking and learning skills: Vol. 2. Research and open questions* (pp. 563–578). Hillsdale, NJ: Erlbaum.

Schoenfeld, A. (1982). Measures of problem-solving performance and of problem-solving instruction. *Journal for Research in Mathematics Education, 13,* 31–49.

Schoenfeld, A. (1983). *Problem solving in the mathematics curriculum: A report, recommendations, and an annotated bibliography.* Report prepared for The Mathematical Association of America Committee on the Teaching of Undergraduate Mathematics.

Schoenfeld, A. (1985). *Mathematical problem solving.* New York: Academic Press.

Segal, J. W., Chipman, S. F., and Glaser, R. (Eds.). (1985). *Thinking and learning skills: Vol. 1. Relating instruction to research.* Hillsdale, NJ: Erlbaum.

Simon, H. A. (1976). Identifying basic abilities underlying intelligent performance of complex tasks. In L. B. Resnick (Ed.), *The nature of intelligence* (pp. 65–98). Hillsdale, NJ: Erlbaum

Sleeman, D. (1983). Assessing aspects of competence in basic algebra. In D. Sleeman and J. S. Brown (Eds.), *Intelligent tutoring systems* (pp. 185–199). New York: Academic Press.

Stein, N. L. (1986). Knowledge and process in the acquisition of writing skills. In E. Z. Rothkopf (Ed.), *Review of research in education, 13* (pp. 255–258). Washington, DC: American Educational Research Association.

Stein, N. L., and Trabasso, T. (1982). What's in a story: An approach to comprehension and instruction. In R. Glaser (Ed.), *Advances in instructional psychology* (Vol. 2, pp. 213–267). Hillsdale, NJ: Erlbaum.

Sternberg, R. J. (1986). *Intelligence applied.* New York: Harcourt Brace Jovanovich.

Sternberg, R. J., and Detterman, D. K. (Eds.). (1979). *Human intelligence: Perspectives on its theory and measurement.* Norwood, NJ: Ablex.

Svenson, O., and Hedenborg, M. (1979). Strategies used by children when solving simple subtractions. *Acta Psychologica, 43,* 477–489.

Thorndike, E. L., and Woodworth, R. S. (1901). The influence of improvement in one mental function upon the efficiency of other functions. *Psychological Review, 3,* 247–261, 384–395, 553–564.

Toulmin, S. E., Reike, R., and Janik, A. (1979). *An introduction to reasoning.* New York: Macmillan.

Tuma, D. T., and Reif, F. (Eds.). (1980). *Problem solving and education: Issues in teaching and research.* Hillsdale, NJ: Erlbaum.

Turkewitz, H., O'Leary, K. D., and Ironsmith, M. (1975). Generalization and maintenance of appropriate behavior through self-control. *Journal of Consulting and Clinical Psychology, 43*(4), 577–583.

vanDijk, T. A., and Kintsch, W. (1983). *Strategies of discourse comprehension.* New York: Academic Press.

Voss, J. F., Greene, T. R., Post, T. A., and Penner, B. C. (1983). Problem-solving in the social sciences. In G. H. Bower (Ed.), *The psychology of learning and motivation: Advances in research theory* (Vol. 17, pp. 165–213). New York: Academic Press.

Vygotsky, L. S. (1978). *Mind in society: The development of higher psychological processes* (M. Cole, V. John-Steiner, S. Scribner, and E. Souberman, Eds. and Trans.). Cambridge, MA: Harvard University Press.

Wales, C. E. (1979). Does how you teach make a difference? *Engineering Education, 69,* 394–398.

Wales, C. E., and Nardi, A. H. (1985). Teaching decision-making: What to teach and how to teach it. In A. L. Costa (Ed.), *Developing minds: A resource book for teaching thinking.* Alexandria, VA: Association for Supervision and Curriculum Development.

Wales, C. E., and Stager, R. A. (1977). *Guided design.* Morgantown, WV: West Virginia University Center for Guided Design.

Weinstein, C. E., and Underwood, V. L. (1985). Learning strategies: The *how* of learning. In J. W. Segal, S. F. Chipman, and R. Glaser (Eds.), *Thinking and learning skills: Vol. 1. Relating instruction to research* (pp. 241–258). Hillsdale, NJ: Erlbaum.

Whimbey, A., and Lochhead, J. (1982). *Problem solving and comprehension.* Philadelphia: The Franklin Institute Press.

Whimbey, A., and Lochhead, J. (1984). *Beyond problem solving and comprehension.* Philadelphia: The Franklin Institute Press.

Wickelgren, W. A. (1974). *How to solve problems.* San Francisco: Freeman and Co.

Woods, D. R. (1983). Introducing explicit training in problem solving into our courses. *Higher Education Research and Development, 2,* 79–102.

Woods, D. R., Crowe, C. M., Taylor, P. A., and Wood, P. E. (1984). The MPS program for explicitly developing problem solving skill. In L. P. Grayson and J. M. Biedenbach (Eds.), *ASEE Annual Conference Proceedings* (Vol. 3, pp. 1021–1035). Salt Lake City, UT: American Society for Engineering Education.

Woods, S. S., Resnick, L. B., and Groen, G. J. (1975). An experimental test of five process models for subtraction. *Journal of Educational Psychology, 67,* 17–21.

Appendix

The following individuals were kind enough to discuss their work or provide materials for study during the course of this project:

RUDOLF ARNHEIM
Ann Arbor, Mich.

A. B. ARONS
Department of Physics
University of Washington

TONY BLAIR
Department of Philosophy
University of Windsor

ALFRED BORK
Professor of Physics
Director, Educational
Technology Center
University of California, Irvine

NEIL M. BROWNE
Department of Economics
Bowling Green State University

COURTNEY B. CAZDEN
Graduate School of Education
Harvard University

MICHAEL COLE
Laboratory of Comparative
    Human Cognition
University of California,
    San Diego

MARTIN COVINGTON
Department of Psychology
University of California, Berkeley

DONALD F. DANSEREAU
Department of Psychology
Texas Christian University

EDWARD DE BONO
Fekenham
Norfolk, England

SHARON DERRY
Center for Educational
    Technology
Florida State University

REUVEN FEUERSTEIN
Hadassah-WIZO-Canada
    Research Institute
Bar Ilan University
Jerusalem

FRANK FISHER
Urban Institute
Washington, D.C.

MAYNARD O. FULLER
Department of Chemical
    Engineering
McGill University

ROBERT G. FULLER
Department of Physics and
    Director, The ADAPT Program
University of Nebraska

RUTH GARNER
College of Education
University of Maryland

ERNEST T. GOETZ
Department of Educational
    Psychology
Texas A&M University

PAUL HAAS
Department of Economics
Bowling Green State University

ANITA HARNADEK
Midwest Publications Co., Inc.
Pacific Grove, Calif.

JULIA S. HOUGH
Director
The Franklin Institute Press
Philadelphia

RALPH JOHNSON
Department of Philosophy
University of Windsor

BEAU FLY JONES
Chicago Public Schools

STUART KEELEY
Department of Psychology
Bowling Green State University

LAWRENCE KOHLBERG
Graduate School of Education
Harvard University

JILL LARKIN
Department of Psychology
Carnegie-Mellon University

DONALD LAZERE
Department of English
California Polytechnic State
    University

MARK LEPPER
Department of Psychology
Stanford University

MATTHEW LIPMAN
Institute for the Advancement of
    Philosophy for Children
Montclair State College

JACK LOCHHEAD
Department of Physics and
    Astronomy
University of Massachusetts

JOHN McPECK
Department of Philosophy
University of Western Ontario

SARAH MICHAELS
Graduate School of Education
Harvard University

FRED NEWMANN
Director
National Center on Effective
  Secondary Schools
University of Wisconsin

RAYMOND S. NICKERSON
Director, Information Science
  Division
Bolt Beranek and Newman, Inc.
Cambridge, Mass.

STEPHEN P. NORRIS
Institute for Educational
  Research and Development
Memorial University of
  Newfoundland

SCOTT G. PARIS
Director, Center for Research on
  Learning and Schooling
University of Michigan

RICHARD PAUL
Department of Philosophy
Sonoma State College

FREDERICK REIF
Department of Physics
University of California,
  Berkeley

MOSHE F. RUBENSTEIN
School of Engineering and
  Applied Sciences
University of California,
  Los Angeles

MARLENE SCARDAMALIA
Center for Applied Cognitive
  Science
Ontario Institute for Studies in
  Education

ALAN SCHOENFELD
School of Education
University of California,
  Berkeley

MICHAEL SCRIVEN
Department of Education
University of Western Australia

IRVING SIGEL
Senior Researcher
Educational Testing Service
Princeton, N.J.

LESLIE P. STEFFE
Department of Mathematics
  Education
University of Georgia

ROBERT STERNBERG
Department of Psychology
Yale University

JOHN SWETS
Chief Scientist
Bolt Beranek and Newman, Inc.
Cambridge, Mass.

STEPHEN TOULMIN
Department of Philosophy
University of Chicago

CHARLES WALES
College of Engineering
Center for Guided Design
University of West Virginia

PERRY WEDDLE
Department of Philosophy
Sacramento State University

CLAIRE E. WEINSTEIN
Department of Educational
  Psychology
University of Texas at Austin

ARTHUR WHIMBEY
Lakeworth, Fla.

MERLIN WITTROCK
Department of Education
University of California,
  Los Angeles

DONALD R. WOODS
Department of Chemical
    Engineering
McMaster University